Gladys,
What can I say,
You're so special.

Jane

The
Indispensables

The Indispensables

Jane Black

HEWITT HOUSE

Old Tappan, New Jersey

The incidents related in this book are true. Some of the names have been changed. That seemed like a good idea.

With thanks for the editorial
assistance of Mary Carey.

Contents

The
Indispensables

1

Unless It Really Hurts, Just Smile!

Great Falls, Montana, never claimed to be the crossroads of the world. Captain Meriwether Lewis did wander through the area in 1805. He did not linger, however. There was some difficulty with a grizzly bear. Besides, he was headed west. There is some discussion about who really founded the town. The wise money goes on Paris Gibson, who arrived in the 1800s. Paris may have founded the town, but he is not the most honored citizen. Charlie Russell is. Charlie Russell, the cowboy artist. There's a Charlie Russell Museum and a Charlie Russell Collection, and by 1963 there were many other things in Great Falls. There were a raft of churches, 55,000 people, more or less, and two television stations. Stewart Hoxworth managed one of the stations.

Stu called me one sleepy September morning just after I'd shoved my kids off to school and my husband off to work. Stu was not exactly Charlie Russell, but he was *somebody* in Great Falls. I put down my coffee cup and the newspaper and sat up straight. If I'd had a little advance notice I would have taken

11

the curlers out of my hair. Thank God we haven't gotten around to putting TV screens on telephones.

"I've got something you're going to love!" boomed Stu. He sounded robust and cheery, the way doctors sound just before they start filling the hypodermic with penicillin.

"Oh?" said I. You can't get into lots of trouble simply saying "Oh?"

"It was done on a local station in New York and it got good ratings," Stu bubbled on. "No reason why we can't do it here. We can get teen-agers from the high schools and you can be moderator. We'll get it in on Monday afternoons—half an hour."

"Half an hour of what?"

"Why, a panel on religion," said Stu, as if that were the most obvious thing in the world. "What say? Want to take it?"

Did I want to take strychnine? Did I want to wade through broken glass in my bare feet? No, I did not. And I said so, loud and clear.

"But with your experience—" Stu protested.

"No. What happens in a Sunday school class happens in a Sunday school class. It happens behind a closed door. You don't want it on TV. Believe me, you don't."

He didn't believe me. He kept on saying things and I kept on saying no, and no, and finally no, no, no. When he hung up my coffee was cold and I'd forgotten where I was in the newspaper. I went upstairs and took a shower and combed my hair, and the day began to go on the way days are supposed to go on. And the day after that and the day after that. Except that Stu kept calling. And at last he came around and rang the doorbell.

He did not bother with hello or nice day or any of those easy openers. "So what does happen in a Sunday school class?" he demanded.

"They talk," I told him.

Stu trailed me into the living room. "That's the idea," he said. "You'd have a pretty dead show if they didn't talk. Look, you've got the most swinging Sunday school class in town, and all you'd have to do is—"

"No," I said.

"Jane, what's the big deal? You advocating human sacrifice or something?"

I said it again. "They talk."

"So?"

"So it's too personal. They talk about themselves. They talk about their parents. They talk about the way they feel. You can't put kids on television and let them go that way. You'd blow the lid off the town."

"I thought Sunday school was about religion." Stu did look puzzled.

"It is. Only religion isn't just a Sunday thing. It's no good if it's just a Sunday thing. And it's tied up with everything   living and parents and love and hate and being jealous and death. Stu, do you know one thing we get to, always, every year? We talk about suicide."

"You've got to be kidding."

"I'm not kidding. We talk about suicide. Not is it wrong to kill yourself and will you go to hell if you do, but we talk about how can you go on living. You wouldn't believe the kids who aren't sure they can."

"Jane, they're just children!"

"That's right. And if a child has a problem, it's a big, big problem. Some of them think it's so big they can't handle it. No way. And no way could you put that on the air."

Stu scratched his chin. "I see what you mean. But you know . . . you know it's a darn shame. I mean, you never hear anything about kids unless they're in trouble. I wanted to show that it doesn't have to be that way."

"Of course it doesn't have to be that way. Most kids are great. And they're so bright you wouldn't believe it. And ideals! And do they ever care!"

"That's what I mean," said Stu. "Look, so we leave religion out of it. Also suicide, please, God. There has to be a way to show the good things. It can't all be about how I can go on living, because they *are* going to go on living. What are they going to do with their lives? They must have plans. They must have opinions about things. They must want things."

"And how!" I agreed.

"So okay, no religion," said Stu. He stood up. "You think about it, okay? Just think about it. And call me."

It was not too much to ask. He had, of course, plopped his project right in my lap, but I did think about it. A few days later I called him.

"We'll need music," I told him.

"Jane, that was not what I had in mind."

"I know, but it's built in. If you have kids you have to have music. And no canned Mantovani. Live. A rock group."

"One half hour of hard rock will do absolutely nothing for us."

"I am not talking about one half hour of hard rock. I am talking about one number or two numbers. And kids doing the numbers."

"And then?"

"And then maybe an interview with some kid who's done something important."

"Okay. That's good."

"And sports. You know, local events. I'm not sure the girls will like it all that well, but the boys will."

"Well, maybe."

"And a TTT thing."

There was a long, choked silence. "TTT?" said Stu.

"You like that?" I was proud of it. "Tips to Troubled Teens."

"I thought you were going to stay away from religion."

"It won't be religion," I told him. "Just kids helping other kids with their problems. Don't knock it. 'Dear Abby' has built a sparkling career on this kind of thing. Could be fun and helpful at the same time."

There was another long silence, then Stu said, "Why not make up a format and bring it in and we'll talk about it?"

"What's a format?" I asked.

"Just write down what you want to do. Outline it. And how long everything will take. Okay?"

Okay. I have never cared much for homework, but okay. I took the cover off my husband's typewriter and wrote things down and wrote things down and imagined interviews and tried to figure how many minutes and how many seconds and finally I went to see Stu.

He bought it.

"Be ready in a week?" he said brightly.

"Argh!" I screamed.

"Ten days?" asked Stu.

We settled on three weeks. It was not enough time. It really was not. In less than a month we had to put together a package. We had to find our permanent teen-age hosts and our permanent rock group. We also needed to line up guests for interviews and for panels; we wanted to have panels.

We started with the schools. They were the logical places, and school principals are reasonably easy to see, especially if you can tell them you're representing a television station. Once you've seen the principals, the head counselors are no problem. The principals simply send for them and they come. We met and we talked. I suppose, looking back on it, that I did most of the talking. I probably sounded like Queen Victoria in a par-

ticularly brisk mood, but I had to be brisk. We had only three
weeks. I put it flat out. I needed the brightest, the sharpest, the
most articulate kids. I had a TV show to do. I needed the best
and I needed them *now!*

Say what you will about bureaucracies—and school systems
are one kind of bureaucracy—but those teachers moved. In
three days I had the kids in my house. There was George—
more than six feet of solid muscle. It was considered clunky to
wear your letterman's sweater that year, so George was not
wearing a letterman's sweater. But you had only to look at him
to know that there was one luring moths to the back of George's
closet. He sat on his shoulder blades and stared at me. He was
curious. He was questioning.

Polly sat on her heels. She was pretty, clear-eyed, shining,
and starched—and apprehensive about the whole thing.

Suzie and Bud didn't sit. They stood off by the fireplace and
twitched.

So I had my permanent hosts. Permanent and worried. Scared
blue, in fact. But excited. The idea of appearing on a TV screen
was too much. Unreal. Outa sight.

I also had my combo. My own kids and their friends had
picked Mark and the Electric Impulses as the most solid rock
combo going. The Impulses installed themselves in the family
room, plugged into various wall sockets, and began to blast out
"Louie! Louie!" They were not nervous. They knew what they
were about.

Hard rock takes some getting used to. The first blare from
the family room lifted me two feet off my chair. I fled to the
kitchen and rattled ice cubes into a bucket and put glasses and
cokes on a tray. Mark and his Electric Impulses were quite as
electric, and quite as loud, in the kitchen.

Back I went to the living room. George was still sitting on
his shoulders. Polly was still sitting on her heels. Bud and Suzie

were still over by the fireplace. But for some reason which adults should not even try to comprehend, that music had had a sort of tranquilizing effect on the four kids. They were twitching, but they were twitching to the beat.

Bud and Suzie did the honors with the cokes and we were ready to talk.

Shout is what we did. You have to shout when you are infested by Electric Impulses.

"They're groovey!" said Polly. "The kids will really dig them. How much will they play on the show?"

I was ready with my format. "We have twenty-eight minutes and thirty seconds for a half-hour show," I yelled. "With three minutes out for commercials and public service spots, we have twenty-five minutes and thirty seconds. With three segments besides music, we could have six minutes per segment, and the Electric Impulses could do two numbers. How does that sound?"

George looked horrified. George was slated to do the sports segment. "You mean I'd have to get athletes to talk for six minutes? They're great guys, but sometimes they aren't exactly articulate."

"Well, hopefully, we'll have film of the sport being featured. Will that help?"

His eyes lit up. "Sure. Okay. Then they could talk about the game, and maybe even explain it to gals or adults who don't understand the sport."

"What's with this Triple-T thing?" Bud said. I had tapped him for Tips to Troubled Teens. He and Suzie. "Is that advice to the lovelorn?"

"Not necessarily," I said. "I see it as an area where kids can write in about problems and—"

Bud went stiff. "That could be dangerous. They could write about everything from what's with the human navel to having a phobia about insects!"

"Everybody has some kind of a phobia," said Polly. "If they hear about other kids having one and you can tell them how to lick it—"

"Suppose we can't tell them how to lick it?" demanded Bud.

"If this segment works out," I said, "I think you should save the more difficult problems, or the ones that require professional help, for a special show. We could get a psychiatrist to come on and help out."

Bud looked greatly relieved.

"What about me?" asked Polly. "What am I supposed to do?"

"Jack of all trades," I told her.

"Meaning?"

"We'll have panels. You can sit in. And we're going to have a live audience. For the first show, anyway, I'd like you to be hostess in the audience. Okay?"

It was okay. And we had quite a bit settled. There was one thing which we did not have settled. We did not have a name for the show.

I had a marvelous list of titles which, in my great wisdom and maturity, I had jotted down: Teen Topics, Teen Time, Teen Talk, Trips with Teens. (LSD wasn't that big in 1963 and you could still mention trips.)

"Being a teen," said George, "is like having leprosy."

"You'll get over it," I promised.

"There has to be some other word," insisted Suzie.

The only other one I could think of was adolescent.

"That is absolutely medical!" cried Polly.

"Like pimples," declared Bud.

"Rotten," said George. "Adolescents are rotten kids. That's what we're supposed to be—rotten kids. We've got one thing going for us, though. We're indispensable."

I stared at him. Indispensable? Slouched there in the corner of the sofa, he looked as indispensable as a used Kleenex.

"I mean, you can't do without us," George explained. "If you didn't have us, where would you get tomorrow?"

Now that was an interesting question. I crossed out all my clever Teen-Talk-Topic-Trip titles and wrote "The Indispensables" on my pad. And Stu Hoxworth bought that. We were in business.

Two weeks later we were on the air.

If the kids had been nervous that first day at the house, they were almost paralyzed that first afternoon at the studio. Oh, everyone knew what to do. I had told them. Smile! No matter what happens, smile! When things go wrong, and they will, smile! And go on. Unless your back is broken or the ceiling just fell on your head, go on. Don't embarrass your audience by being embarrassed.

We did have everything going for us that first day. The studio was too small for the hundred kids we'd rounded up for the audience. It was also too small for Mark and his Electric Impulses, complete with amps. We had to stick the combo way back against a curtain. For the Triple-T set we had a desk which the Salvation Army had refused to take. It was wonderfully effective with three big wooden T's tacked to it. We didn't exactly have a sports set for George's interview, but we had a nice sign, SPORTS, which we put up behind the place where George would sit. It was crooked, but it was there. My interview would take place on the academic set. "Academic" is too long—and too academic—to put on a sign. We settled for dignified simplicity—a table and a couple of chairs.

Ah, yes! We also had a director who, at that point, hated teen-agers. He was only twenty-eight. Probably the memory of thirteen through nineteen was still painful for him. "Impossible!" said he. "You can't *put* this kind of show on the air."

"Smile!" I reminded the kids.

They smiled. We had gotten them sweat shirts with "Indispensables" lettered on the front. They smiled and they sweated on their sweat shirts.

And five, four, three, two, one—we were on.

Our first academic guest was a joy. Her name was Cheryl. She was bright, beautiful, poised, and a National Science Fair winner. She worked in a very select lab under the direction of a pathologist and she did things with mice. She had a mouse named Bill who kept having spontaneous tumors. She had a mouse named Marie who had a transplanted kidney. When Marie made her television debut, she had three tiny, pink baby mice with her.

Cheryl discussed Bill and his tumors, and she talked at length about his thymus. I had looked this up ahead of time so that I could listen intelligently. The thymus is a gland, and it is very important. At least, it was very important to Cheryl and to Bill.

When she had finished with Bill, Cheryl handed him to me, thymus and all.

We were on camera. I smiled.

Bill threw up.

"Cheryl!" I said.

She was busy with Marie. "Don't worry," she said. "He's all right."

Bill threw up again.

"Shall we put Bill back in his cage?" I asked.

"No. Don't worry. He's fine."

Bill then got sick at the other end.

So there I stood with a sick mouse while Cheryl explained all about Marie. Then somehow, someway, one of the cages turned over. For the first time, Cheryl lost her cool. I lost Bill, and Marie got away, together with her babies.

"They're only mice!" yelled Polly, as half the kids started climbing walls. "They're cute little mice, that's all! Just little mice!"

Some guardian angel in the control room threw on a "One moment please!" logo and for sixty seconds we were off the air. George and his athletic guests leaped into the audience and retrieved Marie and one of her babies. Bill wasn't hard to catch. He hadn't been feeling well to begin with, so he hadn't gotten past the second row of seats. I let Cheryl pick him up. Two of Marie's babies vanished from the studio. I hope they fared well. Perhaps somewhere in Great Falls there is a haven for orphaned mice. We didn't have time to worry about it. We were back on the air.

Bud and Suzie came on with their Tips for Troubled Teens. Bud had been scared stiff about how he would read the letters we'd gathered up for the occasion. He read them okay. One was from a girl who was having trouble with her parents. Teens always have trouble with parents. It's universal. The other letter was from a boy who was having trouble with his girl. She was a nice enough girl, but she couldn't keep her hands off him. "She's always climbing my frame" was the way he put it.

"Wheesh!" said Bud. "I should have such problems!" Then he and Suzie were off and running, and for six minutes they talked carefully and thoughtfully about those parents and that girl. They decided that both the old folks and the girl were insecure and needed reassurance. "And hang onto that girl," Bud concluded. "Remember, she's *your* girl."

Then it was time for the commercial. We had a bank sponsoring part of the show. Mark wanted to do the commercial. I hadn't been for this; I thought hard rock was really Mark's thing. But he was so sure he could do a good job and the bank had approved. He had painstakingly memorized the entire message.

He got up; the red light on the camera flashed and he took a deep breath. He smiled. He said, "I'm . . ."

There was a dreadful silence and another smile.

"I'm . . ."

"Mark!" I prompted.

"I'm Mark."

Luckily I had prepared idiot cards with the message written out in huge letters. I grabbed the cards and skidded over next to the camera. If Mark couldn't remember his own name, it was a cinch he wasn't going to recall much about the bank. He smiled, focused on the cards and got through.

By this time, our second camera was jockeyed in on George, and George was waving wildly.

"And now," I said, " 'The Indispensables' bring you sports. Here's George with his sports guests."

The red light on George's camera went on. George stopped waving. He smiled for all he was worth. "I'm here with my sports guests," he started. "Great guys! These are the greatest guys, and they're—they're—"

"Football!" snapped one of George's two huge athletes.

George said, "Football!" Then, having gotten a grip of sorts on the situation, he said, "Guys, we're going to sit down now and talk about . . ."

Two fannies bent toward the chairs on the sports set. George stopped smiling and closed his eyes, and I saw then what all the waving had been about. The chairs on the set were borrowed from "Romper Room." Those football players were not going to make it.

After the chairs had splashed all over the floor—and don't think wood can't splash—George looked down. Again you could see "Smile!" go through his head. He smiled so hard he showed the fillings in his back molars.

The audience broke up.

"Why don't we all sit down, guys, Indian-style, and talk about football?" said George brightly.

They were agreeable. They were already sitting; all they had to do was cross their legs. George joined them and they talked so well that we had to cut them short to get to the combo.

Mark had rejoined his group against that ugly, gray curtain. When he got the cue they turned on, with amps full up. We didn't know, because no one had told us, that you can't broadcast music that way. It had sounded fine when they rehearsed in our family room—a large place with sturdy windowpanes.

The director flew out of the control booth and grabbed me. "Turn that noise off!" he yelled. He had to yell; I can't read lips. "We can't put that kind of sound on the air!"

He was right. The kids in the studio loved the Electric Impulses, but all our friends out there in television land got a horrible buzz. It couldn't be helped. There wasn't any way to adjust the audio, and "Louie! Louie!" blared on.

Then that hideous gray curtain fell on Mark. He was singing tenor harmony when it happened. I'd told everyone to go on, no matter what, so Mark sang louder to be heard through the drape. He may even have smiled. I couldn't see his face. The three wooden T's came clattering off the old desk and the show was over, or almost over. We still had to say good-bye.

We had a one-minute public service spot, which gave the kids time to skitter past the table where Bill the mouse had been so ill. George's lip was twitching as he waded through the splinters of the "Romper Room" chairs. "Close like we're all happy," I told them.

We kicked aside the wooden T's and the red light on the camera flashed.

"Now, George," I asked, "what's coming up next week?"

"Better than this week, I hope," he said.

They turned the cameras on the audience then, and the kids went down and shook hands. Some of them got hugged. We were off the air and everyone was laughing. They were crying, too, laughing and crying.

Two days later we had so much mail that the postman hated us.

In three weeks the show went to a full hour and we had a second sponsor.

So mistakes can be charming.

Also, nothing succeeds like a really well-staged fiasco.

2

The First Sunday

Of course I would never have gotten "The Indispensables" on the air if it hadn't been for the Sunday school class. For one thing, Stu Hoxworth would never have thought of me for a panel show on religion. For another, Bud and Suzie, Polly and George probably wouldn't have trusted me enough to come smiling through the way they did. Because those four students, those four wonderful Indispensable hosts who had been recommended by their schools, were no strangers. I had known each of those kids for three years, and when I first met them they hardly seemed indispensable. They seemed, to quote George, rotten, and they were out to destroy me.

It was Doctor Brownell who got me into the Sunday school class. At some time in his career, James Michener must have wandered through Great Falls and set eyes on Doctor Brownell. He just had to be the inspiration for Abner Hale in *Hawaii*.

"The Junior League is all very well, Mrs. Black," said Doctor Brownell. "Scout groups are all very well. And the PTA, of course. But it is absolutely essential that we have a teacher for the seventh and eighth grade Sunday school class."

He pulled his glasses down on his nose so that he could look over them. I knew who was elected.

"They're divine little people at twelve and thirteen," said the good doctor.

It was a statement that only a childless man could make. I knew better. My Tommy was thirteen. My daughter Jamie, at eleven, was edging toward turmoil. Nine-year-old Jack was still fairly well in hand, but I looked at him and thought of dormant volcanoes.

"They're adolescent angels," said Doctor Brownell. His voice was deep and warm and firm and spiritual. He was very, very wrong, but he sounded very, very right. Could I tell him? Of course not.

"How could you tag yourself with a thing like this?" my husband demanded.

That helped.

"Are you ready?" he asked, that first Sunday morning.

I had had four cups of coffee, one bite of toast, and a nibbling of egg. I was not ready. I would never be ready. I wanted to be sick.

"Is it for real, Mom?" Tommy asked.

"You've never taught Sunday school before," Jamie pointed out. "You're not the type."

"No one is," said Tommy. "Besides, I was in that class last year."

"So?"

"So I know some of those kids. Hey, Mom, could you just . . . sort of . . . well, just not mention me?"

"Yeah!" said Jamie. "This could kill me with some of my friends, too. I mean, not that I care. You're still my mom!"

"Thanks a heap!" I snapped. "Too bad Typhoid Mary isn't around. I'll bet she'd love to take the class."

Jack still hopped about quite a lot. He started hopping now. "I've got it! I've got it!"

"Got what?" asked Tommy.

"Mom can wear that neat, tall new hat! The straw one!"

"But that's a beach hat!" I cried.

"Yeah!" Jack was elated. "You won't look a little bit like a Sunday school teacher."

He whizzed off to get the hat and I remembered my own Sunday school teachers. They had leaned heavily to black hats with purple flowers. Several of them had had two chins. One had had no chin at all, and I had found this terrifying. Maybe Jack was right about the beach hat.

"Shirley Temple teaches Sunday school," said Tommy.

Jamie thought for a second. "Gail Storm," she announced. "No lie?"

They grinned. "No lie."

Then Jack was back with the hat and a hug, and I was off.

Doctor Brownell had given me a teacher's manual and I had studied it. The suggested program for the adolescent angel group was A Welcome, A Prayer, A Hymn, Roll Call, The Lesson (to be read by the teacher), The Collection, and The Closing Hymn. It had seemed to me a trifle stiff, and I had decided that for this first Sunday I would eliminate a few things. Most things, in fact. I would start with the roll call and then simply try to get acquainted. I was operating on the theory that only the most fiendish child will devour a friend alive.

Unfortunately, I was four minutes late. My thirteen angels had drifted into two groups. The girls were at the back of the room, clumped together and giggling. The boys clustered near the windows playing something that looked suspiciously like poker.

I had planned a brisk, dashing entrance, but no one even looked around when I came in. I put my manual and my Bible down on the tired old table that served as the teacher's desk, and I slid into the tired old chair that was the official teacher's chair.

Then I screamed. And I jumped. That stupid straw hat flew off and rolled down the aisle between the chairs.

There are things it is best not to pry into. I never did understand what had happened to the chair. I knew right away, however, who was responsible.

"Best job yet, Bart!" howled one kid.

A very handsome boy stood up and took a sweeping bow.

Someone kicked at the hat and then someone threw it and someone else whacked it with a book. When it reached a pallid, incredibly thin girl, the high crown was completely gone. Only the brim remained, held intact by the grosgrain ribbon. The skinny little charmer picked it up and carried it to me.

"I'm Suzie!" she said. "Your halo, madame!"

"Wear it in good health!" called the boy named Bart. "What's next, Georgie?"

Georgie was still carrying about twenty pounds of extra baby fat, but he had a good face and nice eyes. He gave a hand signal, and the room was filled with soaring paper planes. I caught one and unfolded it. It was made out of a church program.

Paper airplanes cannot kill you. Spit balls cannot kill you, either. I tried not to flinch and I kept repeating these two basic truths.

Then, "QUIET, YOU GUYS!"

It came from a pretty girl with dark, shoulder-length hair. She had climbed up on a chair.

"Come off it, Polly," said someone.

But the yelling stopped and the spit balls stopped. If that was what worked, I'd try it.

"YEAH! QUIET, YOU GUYS!" I shrilled.

Polly climbed down off her chair.

I anchored myself to the desk and glared. "I am Mrs. Black. The welcoming demonstration is now over. Everybody sit down. And if you can't find a seat on your own, I'll seat you!"

They weren't sure I could do it. On the other hand, they weren't sure I couldn't. There was a shuffling and a scraping as overturned chairs were put right. Then thirteen bottoms connected with thirteen seats, and thirteen pairs of eyes stared at me. It would be pleasant to say that they were awed. They weren't. They were only waiting to see what would happen next.

"That was the silliest performance I've seen since I was your age," I told them. "You didn't do one new thing." I picked up one of the paper airplanes. "I could make a better plane than this when I was ten," I told them. "And I'm an expert with the spit ball. And when I went to Sunday school, I had a friend who brought in her Flash Gordon ray gun and sprayed the teacher with ink."

The skinny girl named Suzie poked the boy next to her. "How come you didn't think of that, Bud?" she asked.

Bart looked over at her with complete contempt. "Flash Gordon is for the Geritol set," he told her.

"If you have something to say, let's all hear it, Bart," I invited.

He took the bait. He stood up. "Big deal!" he sneered. "So you've been through the whole bit. What's that supposed to mean? You trying to join the club? You're on the other side of the desk now. You can preach at us and you can tattle on us."

"Yes, and I can be bored, just like you," I came back. I was holding on to my temper, but barely. "There is nothing more boring than a bunch of third-rate gagsters. So you woke up this morning and you knew it was Sunday and you knew you'd have to come here. And what could be drearier than listening to some idiot adult reading ancient tales from the Bible? So right away you hated the day and you hated religion and you hated the idiot who'd be your teacher!"

Skinny Suzie crossed one leg over the other and leaned forward to rest a pointed elbow on a pointed knee.

I warmed up. "I didn't want to be bothered with Sunday school, either," I told them. "And I didn't like this morning. I'm not even sure how much sense it makes to tell you what happened to people who've been dead for thousands of years. When I was your age, I didn't like my parents telling me where to spend my Sundays. Now I'll be glad when it's this afternoon and I can forget about Sunday and Sunday school."

Bart was sitting back in his chair, sizing me up like a defense attorney checking out the jury. "So we're having tell-the-truth day," he said.

"Keen!" from the chunky boy named George. "Free expression!"

"Right!" Suzie was back in it. "Beautiful free expression! Pour out your little heart! Say what you feel. But just try it and you get knocked right into the ground!"

Bart laughed. "Like grow up!" he said. "We hear that all the time. If we're really supposed to grow up, why can't we sit in church instead of Sunday school? Church is no big deal, but it's better than this. This is humiliating!"

Pretty, dark-haired Polly put up her hand. She looked very somber and very serious. "Mrs. Black, Bart and Suzie and Georgie aren't the whole class," she said. "About ten of us have been in this class since kindergarten, and every year Bart and Suzie and Georgie—and Bud, too—pull something like this. They're trying to psych you out so you'll quit."

That took guts.

I sat down gingerly, careful not to lean back in that chair.

"We went through seven teachers last year," said Georgie proudly.

"Is that your record?" I asked.

"Yes," Suzie admitted. "We only got four the year before."

"What was the longest anyone lasted?"

"Four months." It was Bart. "Mrs. Ball stuck for four months. We finished her off with Adam and Eve." Bart began to laugh again. I felt I might choke. Adam and Eve could be hot stuff. I hated to think what a kid like Bart might do with them.

Bart pulled himself together and went on with his story. "One Sunday she told us our next lesson would be on Adam and Eve, and we were supposed to read the story and think about it and come prepared with something to offer on that lesson."

Bud snickered and picked up the tale. "Next Sunday, Bart brought a box and put it on her table. He told her he'd thought about the Garden of Eden and had brought some material on it. And when she opened the box and the snake's head popped up, she let out a yelp and reared back so fast she pulled her sacroiliac."

"She was bent way over when she went out the door," said Bart happily. "We haven't seen her since."

"What would you do if you opened a box and a live snake came out at you?" It was a challenge from Georgie.

"I don't know. I'm not afraid of snakes, but I don't like them much. I guess I would have given it back to Bart."

That damped him down.

"If we're finished with snakes, what would you like to talk about?" I asked.

"No lesson?" gasped Suzie.

"Not today."

"What about next week?"

"That's seven whole days away."

"Oh!" Bart made a fast, angry motion with his hand. "So

that's your bag! We're the problem class in this church, and you've probably got fifteen degrees in psychology. So you're going to write down stuff about us, like evasion and flight from reality and hostility and all that junk."

Bart had all the terms right. But he wasn't thinking straight. "What good would that do?" I asked him.

Polly laughed. She was uncanny. "Bart's afraid you're going to steal his power—you know, with the group."

She was right. Bart was the power. He was first of all. After Bart came George and Bud and Suzie. And Polly, out there in left field. There were eight other kids in the class, but not one of them had said a word.

I glanced down the list of names and found one I hadn't heard from. "Mary?"

A girl in the second row got up.

"What do you think?" I asked her.

She shrugged.

"How long have you been in this class?"

"Since kindergarten."

"How do you feel about what happens between the kids and the teacher?"

"It's neat when they fight," Mary decided. "That snake was neat."

"How do you feel about Sundays when you wake up in the morning? How do you feel about Sunday school?"

"I'd rather play hockey with my brothers."

Georgie straightened up. "Are you a hockey player?"

She didn't answer, but she turned red and there was a glint of excitement in her blue eyes.

"No lie, Mary?" asked Bud. "Do you play hockey?"

"Say!" Bart was suddenly with it. "You've got a couple of brothers who are All-State football, haven't you? Aren't Bow and Jim Belhimer your brothers?"

Mary nodded.

"And they play hockey with you?" asked Georgie.

"Yeah."

"On that pig farm!" snapped Suzie. "Ick!"

Polly came charging to the defense. "It's great out there! I've been."

"How bad does it stink?" Suzie wanted to know.

Bud told Suzie to shut up and Georgie asked if he could go out to meet Mary's brothers. So did Bart, who hadn't heard Mary say a word since kindergarten. "I didn't know you had a tongue!" he told her.

Mary laughed then. They all did. And they all began to talk. They talked and talked and I leaned on my elbows and listened. It went from hockey to football and from football to brothers. From brothers it went to parents. And from there it went to understanding, which was quite natural because, according to Bart, parents never do understand.

"And they don't want us to understand them," he decided.

Even Polly agreed with this. "They act like we're all on the same wave length, but we aren't."

The kids looked at me, daring me to defend my generation. "Well, they've had a lot of experiences," I reminded them. "It's taken them years. And they hope to get the lessons across to you and save you some hard knocks. Sometimes they may try in a sentence or two—"

"You mean they've got no patience," Bart interrupted.

"No, I don't mean—" I began.

But Suzie was up. "My parents scream at my brother and me because we fight, but sometimes they fight so bad I think they'll kill each other. I think example is important!"

Georgie did not agree completely. "My dad's a psychiatrist, and he says fighting is a healthy outlet. You ought to hear him go at it with Mom sometimes."

"Do you like that?" demanded Suzie.

Georgie thought about it. "Sometimes when they do it, I get out of the house," he admitted. "Or I do something bad so they'll be mad at me instead."

"My parents don't fight with each other," said Bud cheerfully. "Battles don't start till the honeymoon's over. My mom's been married a time or three. As soon as the honeymoon's over, she gets a new husband. When you have that many dads, they don't get a chance to know you. That's why they call me Bud. My real name's Everett, but they think that's a mountain or something. Bud's easier."

"So they let you alone." Bart didn't seem to think this was bad at all. "I wish my folks would get off my back. Kids and grown-ups don't get along unless it's a one-way street, and that's the grown-up way. There really isn't any conversation, so there can't be anything but static, like we're having here this morning."

We were not having static and he knew it. His voice dropped and he glared at me. None of the others said a word. He was their leader and they weren't going to turn on him. But they weren't backing him up, either. Not just then.

"Maybe in some cases you're right, Bart," I conceded. "I suppose I've done my fair share of putting kids down. But we've each got to give the other side a fighting chance. At least try to think if they have some justification for what they're saying and doing."

"Sure! It's a gamble," Bud said. "It's a gamble on both sides. Like my mom with each of my new dads. That's always a gamble."

I looked at my watch. It was five minutes after the hour, and I hadn't called the roll yet. I hadn't discussed the Sermon on the Mount, either, but the morning wasn't a total waste. They gave me a chance. They waited while I marked the attendance.

3

After Sunday,
Wednesday Happens

There may be a special corner of heaven reserved for women who are ready for company at 9:30 A.M. If there is, I expect I shall never see it. When my doorbell rang at 9:30 A.M. on the Wednesday after that first Sunday school class, I was where I usually was at 9:30—in my robe and over my second cup of coffee. I decided that whoever it was at the door, I didn't need any. But the bell rang again, and I remembered that the station wagon was standing in the driveway. The persistent bell ringer knew that I was at home. I got up, pulled my robe straight and buttoned the bottom three buttons, which I didn't usually bother with. Then I went to the door and opened it a crack.

"How splendid to find you home, Mrs. Black," said Doctor Brownell.

It wasn't splendid, but I let him in anyway. It is not possible to close the door in the face of a minister.

He followed me into the living room, wavered toward a chair which was stacked with *Mad* magazines, then made for the least cluttered corner of the sofa.

"Coffee?" said I.

"Thank you. I have had mine."

I put the *Mad* magazines on the floor and sat down facing him.

"And how is the lovely family?" he asked.

I wondered if he really knew how many of us there were, but I told him they were fine.

"Isn't it lovely weather?" was the next cliché. "We should be grateful."

It was dark and gray and there was a snappy wind rattling the bushes outside, but I was grateful.

"It's good to see a member of my church surrounded by the comforts of a happy and domestic home life."

What we were surrounded by was a football, a tired sweatshirt that Jack had dropped on his way to bed last night, and several sections of rumpled newspaper.

Having attended to the amenities, Doctor Brownell leaned forward, cleared his throat and got down to the real subject of his call. "I am a little disturbed," he said. "I don't know quite how to approach the subject. I have—er—have heard some good reports on your first Sunday school session."

I thanked him, but I knew that wasn't what was disturbing him.

"I'll get right to the point," he said. "I know you would want it that way. Do you recall, at some time during last Sunday, hinting that parents weren't—er—ah—all that they might be?"

"Good heavens, no!" I said quickly. "Why should I do that? After all, I'm a parent!"

"I am most relieved. You see, Mrs. Black, I had a call from the parents of one of your students. A fine lad. Top drawer parents. It seems he was upset because he felt you suggested that adults, yourself included, didn't allow the youth a fair shake."

My mind raced back over that first Sunday. As I recalled, that discussion had cut both ways.

"I dislike mentioning names," said Doctor Brownell, "but it's most important that you understand the situation. The boy's parents are greatly concerned. They feel that a steady church association is a must. They wish to save him from a repetition of a scandalous situation their oldest son has just put them through."

Then Doctor Brownell, who truly did not wish to mention names, mentioned the name. It was Bart. Bart Wallace. And suddenly it clicked. I don't know why it hadn't occurred to me before. Bart Wallace. He would be the son of Lila and Ellis Wallace. He would be the younger brother of Joe Wallace. And Joe Wallace had indeed gotten into a scandalous situation. A bright boy with a good business head on him, he had recruited a bunch of eager high school girls for interested high school boys. The little agency had been hot and highly successful until someone talked. Someone had to talk. A couple of the girls had gotten pregnant.

"I didn't connect Bart," I told Doctor Brownell. I felt quivery inside and got up to pour myself another cup of coffee.

"The Wallaces are distraught about the situation with Joe," said Doctor Brownell. "They want to be sure nothing like that might happen with Bart."

"I can understand that." I sure could.

"The Wallaces need our help, Mrs. Black," said Doctor Brownell, "and we owe it to them. They give a great deal to the community. And to the church, I might add. They're one of our finest families."

Doctor Brownell took off his glasses and polished them and warned that we must do nothing to undermine Bart's faith in his parents. He then put on his glasses and went on to explain what wonderful people the Wallaces were, with Mr. Wallace on the city council and Mrs. Wallace presiding over four very active women's organizations.

What I wanted to say was "You mean they're never home?" I didn't say it. It would have been unforgivable. In a way, Doctor Brownell was right. The Wallaces were a fine family, or at least a prominent family. Fine families had a right to have fine children. Why not? The children had everything that money could buy. They had the best pediatricians and the best orthodontists, more vitamins and their own TV sets. What I knew, and what Doctor Brownell might not have known, was that sometimes the children of these fine families did not have the things that cost no money—a swat on the tail when they got out of line and someone to listen to them when they got confused. Joe Wallace wouldn't have had a base for his juvenile bordello if there had been a mother really in residence in that big house on the hill.

"I'll do my best, Doctor Brownell," I promised, "but it's going to be ticklish. Bart's a bright boy and he's a leader. He doesn't like having that Sunday school class forced down his throat and he doesn't like having me forced down his throat. He'll try to bomb the whole thing."

"Bomb?" said Doctor Brownell.

"He's already started," I told the minister. "He went home and implied that I said something I really didn't say."

Doctor Brownell ran his fingers through his gray hair. "Are you proposing that we kick the lad out?"

"No. No, I'm not. But he's going to be a handful, and an hour once a week isn't much time."

"You feel he needs discipline?"

I considered Bart. He was not unique. Jamie had come to me once and asked why one of her playmates was allowed to kick her mommie and throw her ice cream on the floor. Bart had all the earmarks of a mommie-kicker, and he had probably thrown his share of ice cream. "He needs discipline," I said. "Badly."

"By you?" asked Doctor Brownell.

"Maybe. No, actually I don't think so. Maybe the other kids in the class could do it. If he pushes too hard, they may put him in his place."

Doctor Brownell looked relieved. "Thank you, Mrs. Black. I knew I could count on you. And Bart's really a nice lad. He's attended our Sunday school for many years and the church has never felt any ill effects from him. He's got to respect you, you know. You're his teacher."

Doctor Brownell got up and headed for the door. I didn't have the heart to suggest that he review the teachers' dropout list for the last few years. Sometimes teachers get a spit ball between the eyes or a snake in a box.

There were no boxes and no snakes the second Sunday. There were the thirteen kids who'd been in the class to begin with plus three new ones, bright with anticipation. Perhaps a Sunday school class where kids could talk about football and parents could out-draw a Sunday school class where kids were told that Mrs. Lot met a dreadful fate because she peeked over her shoulder.

I was more direct on that second Sunday. I called the roll and got that out of the way. I introduced the new kids. And I announced that we were going to sink our teeth into the subject of the life and hard times of Moses. That was in the teacher's manual, and there's some good stuff in Moses. Also, Moses did not have a parent problem; his mother left him in the bulrushes.

Bart groaned. "I told you guys," he said. "What'd I tell you? After Moses we'll have something real wholesome, like toilet training."

Georgie grinned. "Aren't you trained?" he asked Bart.

I could have kissed Georgie, but he would surely have taken violent offense. Bart might be the Big Leader, but Georgie ran him a close second.

Suzie put up her hand. "Do we really need to talk about Moses?" she asked.

Then she hiccupped.

"Yes, I think we do. Moses helped lay the foundation of our religion, and that's what our civilization is based on."

"Moses ran around preaching in his bare feet," sneered Bart. "So is that interesting?"

Suzie hiccupped again.

"I think it's interesting," I said. "He had a lot of radical ideas, and not everyone liked them. Those early prophets took their chances. Some of them were wrapped in animal skins and torn to pieces by wild dogs. Some of them were set afire and used to light the public places."

"Do you really believe that happened?" asked Suzie. And she hiccupped again.

Bud, sitting next to her, poked her with an elbow. "Cut it out, Suz."

It struck me that this was the first sentence Bud had uttered. He had been so vocal last week. And Suzie didn't look a bit well.

She hiccupped again and a ripple of laughter ran through the class. "I can't help it," she said. "It's from last night. And my head hurts."

"Keep quiet!" snapped Bud.

"Well, it's the truth."

"Shut up about it, you nut!" Bud's face got red. Then he hiccupped.

"You're drunk," said Bart.

He was sharp. They were drunk, or at least hung over.

"Not really," insisted Bud. "Not like it sounds. I mean . . ."

"You were too drunk last night," said Suzie. "You were worse than I was and I was falling all over everything. And I feel awful!"

"Why don't you shut up?" He looked as if he would like to murder her.

"I want to tell Mrs. Black what happened, that's all. She'll understand. Can't I just tell you what happened, Mrs. Black?"

"You don't have to tell me anything, Suzie," I said. "In fact, it's better if we forget the whole thing and get on with the lesson. Suzie, do you want to go home?"

"No. I want to tell how we happened to get drunk," She still had a lot of something stirring around in her brain. "We didn't do it on purpose. We didn't know it would happen."

"I don't believe you," said Polly. "No one gets drunk when they're thirteen!"

"That's what you say," said Bart. "I was eight the first time I got drunk and I've been drunk lots of times since. And I smoke, too. It's no big deal."

"But why?" cried Polly. "It's terrible to get drunk!"

"It isn't either terrible. Everybody does it."

Bud agreed in an owlish, alcoholic way. "But the only terrible thing is you feel awful the next day and you have to stay in bed."

Bud wasn't letting me in on a secret. For years I had been on the Sunday station wagon brigade. We picked up the kids who were supposed to get their weekly dose of religion. We picked them up because their parents were too bombed out to drive them.

"Bud's folks and my mother and father gave a cocktail party before the dance last night and that's why Bud and I got drunk."

There! Suzie had managed to get it out.

"You were at the party?" Georgie didn't believe it.

"No, but we were at the house," said Bud. "After they all left for the dance, we finished the booze in all the glasses."

"Don't forget what was left in the bottom of the bottles," said Suzie.

I wished I had brought a couple of bromos. But who would think of bromos for a Sunday school class?

Bud laughed. He might feel wretched, but he still laughed. "That party was a real blast. Congressman Evans was there and he was talking loud about this new bill that's up, and I guess he was making sense. Everybody was listening. Then, POW! He fell flat on his face. It was neat! And when they went to get his coat out of the closet, there was Mrs. Van Buren. She'd shut herself in with her own bottle and a glass and she was passed out colder than a glacier."

"Mrs. Nelson was the funniest one," Suzie said. "She kept coming out to the kitchen to sneak hors d'oeuvres because she's fat and her husband gets mad when she eats too much, and she kept kissing Mary Jo."

"Who's Mary Jo?" asked Georgie.

"She's Tula's little girl," Bud told him. "Tula catered the party and brought Mary Jo because she can't afford a baby sitter. So Mrs. Nelson kept kissing her."

"So?" said Polly.

"Mary Jo's colored, and Mrs. Nelson really, really hates colored people," Suzie said. "Boy, I'll bet she's washing her mouth today, if she remembers."

"She won't," Bud decided.

"That's very interesting," I got in. "Now about Moses . . ."

"Excuse me, Mrs. Black." Bart's voice was taunting. "Shouldn't we be able to talk about things that are important to us?"

"Sure, Bart, but this is getting a little personal—not to say gossipy."

Polly stood up. She looked shocked. "Could we talk about this a little more?" she asked. "I'd like to know how you feel about getting drunk."

"Declare the Fifth Amendment, Mrs. Black," called Bart.

"You're all heart, Bart. Why not drop the Perry Mason role and let me handle my own defense?"

That was fairly dumb of me, because then I had to do it. I knew a lot of those kids had parents who waded regularly and deeply into the giggle water. Was I going to be accused of undercutting parents again?

I chose my words with care. "A lot of people drink moderately at social functions and then are accused of being drunk. Exactly what is drunk?"

Georgie's hand flew up. He was the expert. His dad was a psychiatrist. "You're right, Mrs. Black. My dad says some people have one drink and get loud and talk as if everyone in the room was deaf. Some people get a thick tongue on one drink. Mom and Dad have this one friend who's real quiet and plain, and when she has a drink or two she thinks she's Elizabeth Taylor and she tries to snag all the men. Dad says it's dangerous to drink because you want to be Elizabeth Taylor."

"Are those people your dad's patients?" Suzie asked.

"No. He doesn't talk about his patients. I only know he has some who go to him because they're bad alcoholics. That's wild. I mean, the D.T.'s and straight jackets and that jazz. That's not funny."

"My mom drinks a lot when my dad's out of town," admitted a boy named Charlie. "She says she has to have an outlet or she'll explode. There ought to be better outlets. When she gets swacked, all she does is cry."

"Crying is a good outlet," said Georgie.

"You can cry without drinking," said Polly. "I do."

One of the newcomers, an angelic little soul named Debbie, was of the opinion that drinking was part of the scene, and you'd better learn to drink at home so you could handle it when you got out into the world.

A second newcomer, Harry, believed it was more important

to know when to drink than how. Harry's father was a sales-man. He plied his clients with liquor, but he never touched the stuff himself until the deal was signed, sealed, and sworn to. This, according to Harry, was smart business. "Dad says it's okay to drink when you're grown up, but if you drink when you're on the job you can figure on being a real success as a bum." Harry meditated on this sterling advice. "Maybe it's bet-ter not to drink at all," he decided.

"Maybe it is," said Georgie, the expert again. "My dad says drinking can sneak up on you. He says it begins as a social thing, but it can cause lots of problems besides making you an alcoholic. Like he has to examine people who are up for mur-der and rape and stuff. He says lots of times they aren't bad people at all. They just did something crazy because they were drunk."

I began to be glad we hadn't gotten back to Moses.

Polly made a confession. "Both of my grandfathers died of liver ailments. They drank a lot. My parents don't drink at all; they say you don't have to."

"You mean they never tried?" Bart couldn't believe this. "Not even in college?"

"No."

"Boy, I bet they had a ball sitting in their little dorms reading their Bibles."

"My dad was All-American football," Polly came back at him. "My mom was homecoming queen. So I guess it didn't hurt them too much."

"Do you think it would be better if people didn't drink at all, Mrs. Black?" Suzie asked. She had the air of a girl who already knew the answer. She had been into those bottles the night before. "If you have to go one way or the other, wouldn't it be better to leave the stuff alone?"

Bud didn't wait for me to answer. He had that big head that morning. "It mostly causes problems," he decided. "I mean, it's a risk. If you do it, you're taking a chance, right?"

"You're taking a chance," I agreed.

When the hour was over, Bud and Suzie took their hangovers away with them. The rest of the class filed out. They were not exchanging funny stories about hilarious drunken parents and neighbors. They were somber.

Doctor Brownell called me at exactly one o'clock the following Wednesday. This time he did not want to see me at home. He wanted to see me in his study, and it was terribly important and it was right now.

There were other things I would rather have done, but I went. Doctor Brownell's study was as solemn as the doctor himself. It was lined with heavy tomes on theology and occupied by the minister and four other grim-faced adults. Doctor Brownell introduced me. There was Bud's mother, who was beautiful, and Bud's stepfather, who looked as if he'd be fun to have around the house. There were Suzie's parents. Right then they didn't look as if they'd be fun to have anywhere.

Doctor Brownell, who was great on preliminaries, served tea. I knew I hadn't been invited to sip some orange pekoe and exchange small talk. I helped myself to too much sugar and too much milk and slopped tea into the saucer. I smiled and told Mr. and Mrs. Barnes how much I enjoyed Bud in my class. I smiled and told Mr. and Mrs. Monroe what a bright girl Suzie was.

"She's very vulnerable now, Mrs. Black," said Mrs. Monroe.

That was a dark remark.

Doctor Brownell sidled up to the point of the meeting by saying that the situation was extremely delicate.

"Disgusting might be a better word," said Mrs. Monroe.

I put my cup down on the table. "Would someone please tell me what we are talking about?" I asked.

"Mrs. Black, have you any sense of values?" demanded Mrs. Monroe. "Have you any at all?"

"Now let us not make this sound like a criminal act," said Doctor Brownell.

Mrs. Monroe exploded. "It is a criminal act! We send our children to this woman assuming they will be taught loyalty and respect for property, and integrity, and in one hour she destroys everything! Everything!"

"Control yourself, Tootsie," said Mr. Monroe.

Tootsie controlled herself, but Bud's beautiful mother took the ball and carried it. "Do you know we had the police force out, Mrs. Black?" she demanded. "The entire police force!"

Then Bud's handsome stepfather began to laugh. "It was funnier than hell," he said. "Excuse me, Doctor Brownell."

"You didn't think it was funny when it happened!" snapped Mrs. Barnes.

"That was because I wanted a drink and there wasn't any. Bud took care of that."

"Bud took care of what?" I asked.

And then I found out. The Monroes and the Barneses had arrived home from a party the night before and had gone to the cupboard or the bar or the cellar or wherever the bottles lived, and there weren't any. There were none in the Monroe house. There were none in the Barnes house. There was no Scotch, no wine, no brandy, no gin, no anything. There wasn't so much as a can of beer. The two couples had decided that a burglar with a monumental thirst had passed their way, so they summoned the law. The officers had spread out to search the properties and had quietly and quickly solved the mystery of the vanishing spirits. The trash cans in the alley behind the houses were crammed full of broken bottles, and the alley itself smelled like Tammany Hall at the tail end of election night.

It was easy to understand Mrs. Monroe's remark about values. The hootch which had gone down the alley drain had cost in the neighborhood of $900. And it was Bud and Suzie who had dumped it, and all because of some silly discussion in a Sunday school class.

"I'll bet you're amused no end with some of the things the youngsters say in your class, Mrs. Black," said Mrs. Monroe.

"I am not amused." I snapped it at her. "I'm fascinated, yes. But not amused. Not by what they say, and not by what they do sometimes."

"Now exactly what is that supposed to mean?"

She didn't know. Of course she didn't know about Suzie and Bud and their Sunday morning hiccups. Suzie and Bud and the class had taken care of that situation. I was sure I wouldn't have to confront another pair of hung over kids. I decided I wouldn't tell her.

"The children talk very openly among themselves," I said. "Sometimes they're upset by things they see. They've been taught to want an ideal world, and they're beginning to realize that they're not living in one. It frustrates them."

Doctor Brownell cleared his throat. "Perhaps what Mrs. Black is trying to say is that children do not always put things in perspective," he interpreted. "Perhaps your children were— er—concerned." He looked away from them, up toward the top bookshelf.

Mrs. Monroe gasped. She opened her mouth to say something, but Mr. Monroe took her by the arm. "Come on, Tootsie. I'll buy you a drink on the way home if you want one."

She pulled her arm away. "What will Doctor Brownell think?"

"He'll think what he thinks already," decided Mr. Monroe.

The four of them went out and left Doctor Brownell and me to our tea.

"Mrs. Black," said Doctor Brownell, "I don't know what this year will bring." He looked very weary. "I don't know what, but I'll take a chance on you."

4

Davie Makes a Difference

The third Sunday we had twenty kids enrolled in the Sunday school class, plus two guests—the Julian twins. They were Bart's contribution to the general excitement. They were avowed atheists, not because they were atheists at all, but because Mommie and Daddy were atheists. They came primed to destroy the whole idea of religion, meaning a belief and reliance on a power greater than your own. It turned out to be uphill work. Jacques and Pierre Julian were two of the most dapper, attractive kids I've ever known, but they couldn't get through a sentence without quoting their father, who was a psychiatrist. So Dad was the word for God to those kids. And according to Dad, religion was a superstition based on fear and only on fear. It was fear of hell, mainly, which neither of them believed in. It was also fear of the unknown. Religion was the same as believing in omens and witches and spells, and being afraid to walk under ladders or open umbrellas in the house. Jacques had what he thought was the crushing argument. He pulled a paper out of his pocket.

"My mom's got all these relatives in Ireland," he told the

class. "They're poor and they're really stupid, and my mother sends them clothes and money. They write to us and it makes us sick to read their letters, but my dad says to keep a sense of humor and pity the poor idiots."

"I have relatives in Ireland and they're not idiots," said Mary.

This bounced off Jacques without making a dent. He unfolded the paper.

"If that's a personal letter to your mother . . ." I began.

He ignored me.

"Dear Cousin Jeanne," he read. "Your welcome letter, check, and package came and we thank you very much for all of it. We had five Masses said for you, your dear mother, and your lovely twins.

"You are doing well in America. God bless you. I hope you will not be putting on airs and forgetting your relatives in your native land. Your cousin Hughie was hung at Londonderry last week for killing a policeman. God rest his soul, and may God's curse be on Jimmy O'Leary the informer and may his soul burn in hell, God forgive me.

"There's not much more to be reporting, but may God bless you and may he keep reminding you to keep sending the money and clothes to keep you from his curses and sudden death. Your devoted cousin, Timothy."

There was some appreciative laughter. Jacques Julian beamed, folded his letter, and sat down.

"That is a lie!" said Polly.

The class was very quiet.

Polly stood up. "It's a lie, and it isn't even an original one. You copied that letter out of a book or something. Anyway, you copied the bit about Hughie getting hung in Londonderry. I've read it before. It's supposed to be funny. Well, I don't think it is. And if anybody was ever stupid enough to write a letter like that, really, it wouldn't prove anything about faith. That's just blackmail."

Polly sat down. The Julian kid opened his mouth and then closed it again, and that Sunday we got all the way through the lesson in the teacher's manual. The Julian kids did not argue further.

But the following Wednesday I had a call from Doctor Brownell. He talked about tradition and harmony in the church. He talked about faith. Finally he talked about the Julian kids.

"They didn't win any points on atheism," I told him.

"We can't chance dissension," he insisted. "We don't want arguments and questions."

"We have questions, Doctor Brownell," I told him. "That's what adolescence is all about. They question everything."

Doctor Brownell sighed.

"I don't think the Julians will come back to the class," I told him weakly.

"I dread the calls that come to me on Mondays and Tuesdays," said Doctor Brownell. In a way it was a personal confession, and quite out of character for the minister.

I was sorry. He was a good man.

The following Sunday, the Julian kids were back.

I was five minutes early for a change, and when I charged into the classroom I saw thirty backsides hanging from the five windows that ran across the west wall. The kids were fascinated by something that was taking place down on the street.

"Boy, that's the neatest car I've ever seen." That was Bart.

"Who's that with her?" asked Suzie.

"It's the chauffeur, idiot," snapped Bud.

"Abba-dabba-doo!" howled Georgie.

"Rats!" said Suzie. "That dress would be too tight for a doll."

"I wish I looked like that," said Mary.

I slammed the door to let them know I was among them and

sat down at the teacher's desk. I called the roll, added eight more names to the list of students and noted the presence of the Julians. Then the door opened and we had yet another new member of the class.

One could understand all the staring out of windows. The girl was trim. She looked like a well-developed sixteen, which was too old for that class. She had enough blonde hair to keep any three ordinary girls happy, and she had enormous blue eyes and perfect features. Her dress was not really too tight, but it fitted extremely well in all the places that a dress should fit.

"Are you Mrs. Black?" she asked. The voice was low and husky.

"That's right."

"I'm Davie Sawyer. The attendance office said I belong in your class."

"What for?" I asked. It was not a bright question, but I had not been prepared for Davie Sawyer.

"I've come to worship with you," she said.

"Ick!" said Suzie.

Bud poked her.

Mine not to question the attendance office. They doubtless knew things that I didn't. I wrote the name down on my list and suggested that she take a seat—any seat.

There were empty chairs in the outside aisle. She went to one of these, swinging her perky little yellow bag as she walked. When she sat down she put the bag on the floor. Then she bent her head and closed her eyes. She seemed to be meditating.

There was a stir among the girls. Several twitched at their own hair or tugged their skirts straight. The boys gaped, speechless and motionless. All except Jacques Julian. "What a sexy broad!" he exclaimed.

The blonde head shot up, then dropped again. In that little moment I saw tears.

"It seems we have a bit of everything represented here today," I said, "including rudeness."

Jacques swallowed. "I didn't really mean that. I—I say things that sound awful sometimes, but I'm only kidding. Tell her, Bart."

"You said it," said Bart. "You tell her."

Jacques looked at Davie. "I didn't mean it," he said.

The blonde head nodded. Without words, Davie was accepting the apology.

I found myself thinking that Davie would probably have a hard time in this class. She would probably have a hard time all through her life. I wished that someone—Polly, perhaps—would move over and sit next to her. But even Polly, special as she was, didn't do it. Davie was too much too soon. She was too beautiful. Davie was the enemy.

Pierre Julian put his hand up. "I hope you don't mind that Jacques and I came back again this Sunday," he said. "It wasn't at Bart's invitation." He flashed his handsome grin. "Just to show you the respect we have for your way of thinking, we borrowed a Bible from a friend and read over the lesson you said you'd cover today."

Davie, curious, slid around in her seat so that she could look at Pierre.

He held up a white leather Bible for all to see, then smiled again and sat down. It was a beautiful performance, but too much for Georgie. He guffawed.

Davie should not have attempted to play the game without first learning the ground rules, but she didn't realize this. She fixed her clear blue gaze on Georgie. "Ah think you're perfectly horrible," she said. "How can you laugh when someone shows such beautiful humility?"

"Would you rather I threw up?" asked Georgie.

"Ah do declare!" said Davie.

The accent was deep Deep South. I frowned, trying to remember if she had talked that way when she first came in.

"Mrs. Black?" said Davie.

"Never mind," I said. "I declare, too. I declare a brief period
of quiet so we can get into this lesson."

We did. It was the story of David, one of the greatest charac-
ters in the Bible. We were well into it, and the kids were listening intently, when Pierre Julian dropped his bomb.

"How about Bathsheba?"

Now there is this thing about Bathsheba and you can't deny
it. They lacked public relations men in Biblical times, so they
tended to get hung up on telling the unvarnished tale.

"Isn't it a fact that David got Bathsheba pregnant while she
was still married to—to—"

"Uriah," I said softly.

"Right. And isn't that called committing adultery?"

"That's right. For nonbelievers, you read the Bible very well.

"So this big good guy was a bad guy, too."

"Who isn't?" demanded Bud. "Look at old Peter. He got
sore when they came to arrest Christ and he cut the ear clean
off one of the guards."

"Do you think it'd be fair to ignore all the years David did
so much for his people and just remember that he fell in love
with another man's wife?" Polly asked.

Then Jacques did a strange thing. He may have been rattled
by the opposition he and his twin were facing. He leaned toward
Polly and said, "I'm surprised *you* approve of this guy David!
You're so chock-full of virtue I'll bet you think girls should
still be virgins when they get married!"

The whole class gasped. Georgie did more than gasp. He went
into a rage. He lunged out of his chair and grabbed the Julian
kid. "Don't you recognize a lady?" he demanded. "Or has your
ego got you too freaked out for that?"

Georgie was shorter than the Julian boy, but he carried more
weight. Jacques shrank. Georgie let him go after a second, but
the Julian boy didn't let go of his subject. King David had com-

mitted adultery and adultery is fascinating. Love affairs are fascinating. And many folks have affairs—not only in the Bible, but right there in Great Falls. It looked as if we were off again on one of those round-table deals when someone said the word *sex*.

Davie turned pink, then white, and then pink again. Now she reared in protest.

"Ah'm shocked to the point of faintness!" she cried. "Ah think sex is dirty and vulgar and Ah've never, never talked to anybody about it in mah whole life and Ah think it's just terrible—terrible—to talk about it in a Sunday school class. Of all places!"

There were worse places—much worse—but one couldn't explain this to Davie. She might look like Miss Junior Playmate of the Year but she wasn't having any.

The Julian kids apologized.

Bart apologized, though it's hard to say for what.

Even Georgie apologized, and he hadn't done a thing.

We got back to King David, skirting the more questionable phases of his story, and for the first time I was spared the usual Wednesday call from Doctor Brownell. Evidently sex was not discussed in any of the students' homes following that lesson.

The next Sunday Davie came to class attired in a fetching lavender knit outfit with a purple bow at the neck and accessories carefully chosen to blend. She paused at my desk on the way in to remark that she hadn't meant to cause a scene in the class the week before. "Ah show my emotions and sensitivities more than most," Davie confided in her low-pitched drawl. "Mumsy tells me this all the time. That's why she feels a Sunday school is so needed for me. It can give me so much strength Ah seem to lack."

She glanced around. Polly was watching her. Their eyes locked for a second and then Polly looked away.

Davie went and sat down alone in the outside row and bowed

her head. Perhaps she was praying for strength to face what would come in the next hour.

Out of due respect for that beautiful bundle of tender emotions and delicate sensitivities, nothing was discussed in the next hour that would upset Davie. No one mentioned S—X once, and we got through Solomon in fine style without dwelling on extra wives or what might have happened with the Queen of Sheba.

Davie stopped after class and thanked me. "I thought you'd all, you know, preach a sermon," she said.

"No, our minister does that," I told her.

"Oh," she said. "This class isn't anything like I thought it would be."

"Nor I," I told her.

Polly started out and Davie hurried after her. She could not, however, hurry enough to catch Polly. Polly walked fast when she had a mind to.

Poor Davie. Whatever Polly had, Davie wanted it. Or she wanted to know the secret. Or maybe she simply wanted to be friends. If only she hadn't been that lovely.

At any rate, I congratulated myself that I wouldn't be hearing from Doctor Brownell that week. The attitude toward Solomon had been impeccable. Davie did make a difference.

5

The Lord Giveth ....

Davie had not been long in the class when there was a week in which Wednesday happened on Thursday. The telephone rang in that black hour before dawn, and when I picked it up, a familiar voice said, "May I come out to see you now, Mrs. Black?"

No one, not even Doctor Brownell, comes visiting before cockcrow. I decided I was dreaming. "No," I said, and put the telephone back on the cradle.

It rang again, immediately. "Are you there?" said Doctor Brownell. "May I come out to see you? Mrs. Black, are you up?"

"No, I am not up." I fumbled the light on and squinted at the clock. "Doctor Brownell, do you know what time it is?"

"Mrs. Black, it is not my practice to call people at 5:40 unless—unless—" His voice, which had been very firm, shook and broke.

I was up. "What is it?"

"An accident," he said. "A terrible accident. Mr. and Mrs.

Miller. Fatal for both of them."

"Polly's parents?"

"Polly's parents. It happened about fifty miles from here."

"Does Polly know?"

"No. Nor does the housekeeper. Mrs. Black, I would be grateful for your help."

He didn't need to be grateful. He had it, for whatever it was worth. I set the alarm so my own family could get up and cope with the morning on their own terms. I put corn flakes and milk on the kitchen counter, fixed the coffee pot, left a note for my husband, and at seven Doctor Brownell and I were ringing the bell at the Miller house.

Polly was up, but fortunately at the other end of the house getting ready for school. Doctor Brownell had first to break the bad news to Tessie, who had kept house for the Millers since before Polly's birth. Tessie's legs literally folded under her, and Doctor Brownell was just in time to snatch at her and guide her into a chair. I was afraid that she was going to scream or become hysterical, but she didn't. She cried quietly, dabbing at her eyes with a man-sized handkerchief she pulled from her apron pocket.

I went into the kitchen and made coffee and put things on the table. One kitchen is apt to be quite like another. I could manage. At least, I could manage breakfast.

Polly skidded in, all morning radiance and shining hair, and poured herself a large orange juice. She was surprised to see me and Doctor Brownell sipping miserably at our coffee, but she wasn't upset. For some reason, she connected our appearance with the fact that her parents were coming home that day.

I wanted to run away.

"Please, child," said Doctor Brownell, "sit down. I must talk to you."

She sat down, but she didn't look at the minister. She looked at me. I couldn't look back. I tried staring at Doctor Brownell, but that didn't help, so I looked out the window.

For once Doctor Brownell kept the preliminaries to a minimum. He told her with amazing gentleness, and he kept his voice calm, though his hands were shaking. After he told her, he stopped talking.

She sat and picked at the green place mat in front of her. "It isn't true," she said at last.

I swallowed hard several times. Then I was able to say, "Your grandmother and your aunt and uncle will come this evening, Polly. They're on their way now."

"Do they know?"

"They know," said Doctor Brownell. He put one hand on hers and began to recite short verses from the Bible. She wasn't listening, but there was something comforting about that low voice droning on and on, saying the good, true things. I kept waiting for her to cry, as Tessie had, or perhaps to faint. She did nothing.

It was the minister who cried, finally, and Polly's pretty face twisted in torment. She got out of her chair. "Please, please don't cry," she begged him.

He shook his head, then stood, patted her hand, and hurried out of the kitchen.

"Will he be all right?" Polly asked me.

"He'll be all right." I wasn't worried about Doctor Brownell just then.

Polly took my cup of cold coffee, emptied it and poured a fresh cup for me.

"Are your parents alive?" she asked.

A frightening temptation came over me. I wanted to say no, so she could relate. But I couldn't.

"Yes," I said.

"Are they old?"

"Not very."

"Do you love them?"

"Yes. Yes, I love them."

"Yes," she said. Then, "If you suddenly found out they weren't—they weren't—" She stopped and pulled at a lock of her hair. "How would you feel?" she asked.

"I guess I wouldn't believe it. Not right away, anyhow."

"It would be a dream, wouldn't it? A bad dream?"

"At first. But later—"

She interrupted. "Would it be terrible for me to go back to bed and sleep . . . and maybe when I wake up . . ."

But there was to be no sleep for Polly that day, and no escape. Only God knows how Suzie got there so quickly, but she did, her eyes three times their normal size in her thin face.

Suzie talked about seeing the pictures in the morning paper, and she cried.

Polly didn't cry.

Suzie confessed that she had always been a little jealous of Polly. She hugged Polly and she cried some more.

Polly told her it would be all right.

Before we managed to get Suzie out the door, the woman who lived across the street appeared. Then there was a friend of Polly's father and a woman who had been on several committees with Polly's mother. Bud came. Bud's mother came. Both of Mary's parents arrived. They were dressed in their Sunday best and Mary's mother carried in a huge casserole. The living room filled up with people and with flowers. The kitchen filled up with food. Women wept. Men cleared their throats.

Polly never cried.

Polly stood straight. She talked to everyone. She comforted everyone. She never cried.

The day was unreal. Tessie recovered enough to make coffee and to wash endless cups. I recovered enough to take telephone messages and to sign for flowers. By late afternoon Doctor Brownell had recovered enough to go to the airport to pick up Polly's grandmother and her aunt and uncle.

There were hugs and kisses when the relatives arrived. They cried and Polly patted them on the shoulders. There was some soft-voiced conversation with Doctor Brownell—arrangements for the funeral—and at last he left, taking me with him.

"She's being very brave," said Doctor Brownell.

"She's being too brave," I told him.

He let me out in front of my house. Everyone could have fried eggs for supper, I decided. I had been planning to shop that day, but there were eggs in the refrigerator.

The house was neat when I came in. There were no footballs or baseballs or bats or twist boards in the living room. There were no batons or pop bottles in the family room. In the kitchen there were three somber kids sitting in utter silence around the breakfast bar.

I washed my hands and took the electric skillet out of the cupboard. "I don't hear your radio, Tommy," I said. It was always blasting at ear-splitting level when he was home.

"I thought you might like it quiet today," he said.

"I'm glad you're home, Mom," said daughter Jamie.

Jack opened a drawer and began to put place mats on the breakfast bar. Then the three of them gathered around and watched me break eggs into the skillet. They were as fascinated as if I had invented chickens. I didn't usually have such an audience, since cooking isn't my favorite part of a meal.

"Will you go back to Polly's tomorrow?" asked Jack.

"I don't think so," I told him. "Her grandmother and her aunt and uncle are with her."

"Will she be okay, Mom?"

"It was a rough day," I told him. "Tomorrow will be rough, too, and a lot of days after that. I hope she'll be okay."

"I'm glad," said Jack. "Don't go tomorrow. It was creepy having you there."

I turned the eggs. Children. For children, the sun always

rises, Dad buys your shoes and pays the bills, and Mom's made out of unbreakable metal. And if anything happens to upset this natural order of things, it's the end of the world.

"Is Polly going to kill herself?" Jack asked suddenly.

The question made me shiver. There must have been a lot of talk at school. "Would that help?" I asked him.

"But without her mom and dad . . ."

"Well, how would her mom and dad feel if, after all the years of loving Polly and caring for Polly and raising Polly to be a fine, strong girl, she suddenly killed herself?"

Jack thought about this. "You and Dad would really whomp me if I did that, wouldn't you?" he asked.

"Like you've never been whomped before!" I told him.

He shut up and ate his eggs. The next day, Friday, I didn't go to Polly's, but there were floods of telephone calls at our house. The funeral was on Saturday and everyone went.

After Saturday there was Sunday and a Sunday school class. I arrived early and sat alone in the big classroom. After a time Davie drifted in. She said good morning, barely, and took her accustomed place in the outside aisle.

We waited. The hour came and went. We were nearly at fifteen after when Davie said, "Maybe they won't come today."

But they did come. They came in a rush, all together. The door opened and they all poured in and I gasped. They looked dreadful and they smelled like—well, they smelled like something I didn't want to meet—ever!

They were bearing flowers.

Suzie was first with a bunch of white mums. They had once been lovely, but whatever wringer Suzie had been through, they had accompanied her.

Bud was behind Suzie, smudged and soiled and carrying a small bouquet of red roses.

The two kids put the flowers on the table in front of me. The rest of the class clumped up behind them, and they explained.

All of them—the entire class, excepting Davie—had been to Polly's house that morning. The mums were for Polly. The roses were for me. They had missed Polly. She had already left for church with her aunt and uncle.

"I'm sure she'll appreciate the thought," I told them. "How did you all get to Polly's?"

"In my dad's truck," said Mary. "The one he uses when he ships the pigs. We could hardly all squeeze in."

That accounted for the smell.

Doctor Brownell came into the room then. It was the first time that year he had so much as opened the door. His eyes fell on the flowers.

"Mrs. Black was so good to Polly," said Bud defensively.

Doctor Brownell nodded. He had also been good to Polly, but it did not offend him that no one had brought him wilted roses. He did not seem to notice the smell.

"The Lord giveth and the Lord taketh away," said Doctor Brownell. "There are times when we cannot help but question —when it is difficult to try to get a grasp on His motives. The Lord's, that is." The old minister pulled out his handkerchief and blew his nose. "Bishop Warner is preaching the sermon this morning," he told them. "I'll go back to Polly and see what I can do to help her. And I hope all of you can find it in your hearts to pray for her. She needs it very much."

He made for the door. At the last moment he stopped and looked at that bunch of wrinkled, smelly kids. "Perhaps," he decided, "it would be better if she were here with you."

He went out.

"Mrs. Black, he's worried about Poll," said Bud.

"Is she really going to be okay?" wondered Suzie.

Playing oracle is not easy. I didn't have much time, which was just as well. Polly came in. She looked thinner, and there were dark circles under her eyes. But she was smiling. Lovely, dry-eyed Polly.

"Do you know we've been trying to see you for over two hours?" Suzie said.

"We went all the way to your house in a pig truck," Bud told her.

"You guys look awful," said Polly.

She liked the mums, even though they did smell more like pigs than like flowers. She liked the present the Julian kids had brought her—a little white music box. When she opened it, a tiny angel popped up and rotated to the tune of an old hymn.

"It's nothing," said Pierre Julian. "We got it out of a box of crackerjacks."

They were beautiful kids. They were dirty and rumpled and smelly, but they were beautiful, beautiful kids. I loved every one of them.

Davie, who hadn't been invited on the great pig truck ride, sat quietly and watched Polly. There was something in her face that I had not seen there before.

Polly called me that night. She sounded as if at last she was going to crack. "Mrs. Black, it's Davie," she said. "She wants to see me. She says she's going to melt into a nervous breakdown if I don't talk to her. Mrs. Black, I don't want to."

"Oh, dear Lord!" I said.

"Mrs. Black, can I come to your house? I mean, will you let me, and I can see Davie there?"

"Well, of course, if you think it will help, but—"

"Thanks, Mrs. Black. I'll be right over."

The telephone clicked, and not long after, the doorbell rang. It was Polly. She'd been running.

"The chauffeur's bringing Davie," said Polly.

"Okay," I told her. "Just remember, Davie's a very emotional girl. If she gets too much for you, let me know, will you, Polly?"

"I will," she promised.

We heard tires on the drive outside. Then Davie was with us. She had dressed for the occasion. This was, somehow, typical of Davie. From some obscure corner of her wardrobe she had resurrected a loose middy blouse and a dark skirt. Her blonde hair was caught back with a bow.

She looked at me and then at Polly. Immediately tears welled up in her eyes. "I may cry a little now and then," she said, "but if you'll be patient with me, I've got some things and I hope maybe they'll help Polly."

There was no trace of a southern accent.

"I have to say this quick, or I won't be able to say it at all," said Davie. "Polly, you have so much to be grateful for!"

Polly backed away from her and sat down on the sofa.

"You've got friends," said Davie. "You've got so many friends. And you had your parents, Polly. I'm not exactly sure how to put this into words, but it seems that if you leave your child something you've really worked at building for her, that's the most important thing."

Polly started to get up again, but Davie waved her back.

"No, wait!" she cried. "I don't mean money. That's what you're thinking, but I don't mean money. I mean, your parents really loved you, Polly."

Polly did not move.

"I've never been loved in my life," said Davie. Then she began to cry in earnest. "I don't mean money. I hate money. You know how my mother gets her money? She gets it from the man she lives with. You know how I got my southern accent? The man she used to live with had one and we were supposed to please him. I hate money and I hate sex and I hate the way I look. My mother picks out my clothes. And the only reason I go to Sunday school is because Jake thinks I should."

"Jake?" Polly was stunned.

"He's the chauffeur. He works for the man my mother belongs to. He's a real good man—Jake, I mean—and he's got five kids of his own. I didn't want to go to his church because they say alleluia and amen, and I didn't want to do that. So he let me pick my own church and I picked yours because it was right there. Nobody knows I go. My mother sleeps late on Sundays. Polly, your mother didn't sleep late on Sundays."

That was crashingly unimportant, but she made her point. Polly moved over and put her arms around Davie. "You're right, Davie," she said. "They did give me everything. That's what I've got to remember."

Davie wept some more and hugged Polly and then, oh glory, Polly began to cry.

We went through heaps of tissues that night. I have never felt it could be put to better use. After the flood of tears, there was cocoa, and then, bless the children, there were even a couple of laughs.

It was late when I stood at the front door and watched the girls go down toward the limousine parked in the driveway. I didn't see Jake clearly. I only got a glimpse of a wide, white smile in a black face as he opened the door for them.

6

A Ham Amid the Blackfeet

The year roared on, and so did that first Sunday school class. By January the enrollment reached sixty and the attendance office decided that sixty was the limit. They had no choice. You couldn't put more than sixty chairs in that room. Polly was able to stay. Her aunt and uncle moved to Great Falls to be with her until she finished high school. The Julian kids never formally enrolled, but they always came. Davie recovered gracefully from her southern accent. She also stopped displaying her delicate and sensitive soul. Bart continued his harassing tactics, but he gradually lost his following as Georgie, and then Bud, lined up with Polly to put him down. And where Bud went, Suzie went. By the end of the year Bart was pretty much alone, except for an occasional boost from the Julian kids. Then the summer came and Sunday school ended for the year; the kids went their ways, separately or in groups.

The next fall, there was a new bunch of kids in that class— and a few of the old ones. Polly, Georgie, Bud, and Suzie didn't come back. They sat in the church. So did Davie. Jake brought her faithfully every Sunday.

You never really lose track of anyone in a town the size of

Great Falls and I didn't lose track of the kids. Polly and Georgie made it easy; they dropped in on me at odd times. Sometimes Davie came with Polly. They'd sit in the family room and consume mountains of potato chips and a fierce dip which combined shrimp and seasonings in proportions that made everyone's eyes water. It wasn't the same as having them in class, but I liked it. I made sure I was always stocked with shrimp. Then "The Indispensables" came into being and we blundered through that first frantic show. It was, in a way, like having the kids in class again. And we were all learning.

I will not stand up before everybody and say that Polly and George, Bud, Suzie and Mark became pros overnight. They didn't. But after a couple of months they were no longer paralyzed when a show began, and they had learned the signals which were delivered by the cameraman. A finger crooked did not mean that the man had arthritis; it meant that the Indispensable had thirty seconds to finish whatever he was doing. Hands held together, then stretched out horizontally, meant slow down, we've got time to fill. A chopping motion across the throat meant hurry it up.

Mark got the signals straight quicker than anyone. He got over his stage fright quicker than anyone. He went through a period of poised competence. Then, right before our eyes, he turned into a complete ham. This has happened to better men than Mark, and I don't hold it against him, but it was a nuisance.

We were two months into the season, and Mark was enjoying himself tremendously, when we received a fan letter in verse. It was anonymous, but not fearfully so. It read:

> TV is a mouse
> And White Man's a bear.
> Uncle Sam is a louse.
> Your show's unfair.

It was signed "A student at Browning High."

Browning I knew. It is the trading center for the Blackfeet Indian Reservation and 90 percent of the population of Browning were Blackfeet. I didn't know what we had done to upset that Browning High student and I was curious enough to want to find out, so I sent a note to the principal at Browning High. I told him about our new youth program on television. I suggested that some of the youngsters in his school might care to participate.

The answer came by return mail. "We would like very much to participate on 'The Indispensables.' Please inform me as to exactly what you would like and I will comply." The note was on the stationery of the principal's office and it was signed by Guy Many Tall Trees.

You can't order a cast for a television show the way you'd order a crate of eggs. You have to talk things over first. I tried to call Mr. Many Tall Trees on the telephone, but the school secretary reported that he was in class and couldn't be disturbed. I said I could drive up the following Wednesday and talk with Mr. Many Tall Trees. The woman on the telephone choked slightly and said that if I wanted to see Guy it would be better to arrive at noon or after three. I promised to make it by noon of the following Wednesday, and I hung up thinking that she was behaving in a most unprofessional manner, calling the principal by his first name.

The following Wednesday I journeyed to Browning, but because of a flat tire along the way I did not get there before noon. I got there at two and drove down the main street. The Blackfeet have fought to maintain their own standards and their pride, and Browning is a fine and thriving place. I knew that about 70 percent of the kids who entered Browning High finished and got their diplomas. Almost half of these went on to college. They didn't all finish and get their degrees, but they sure tried. It was important. Most of them wanted to get into government work so that they could help their people.

Browning High was off the main street: a brick building, fairly new, and with enough lawn and landscaping to insure a leisurely, academic look. Inside the building things were not leisurely. Classes were changing and I had to stand back against a wall while tall bronze boys and short bronze girls streamed past. The kids looked marvelous. The boys ran to broad shoulders and almost no hips, and the girls were so starched that they fairly crackled as they walked. I admired the high cheekbones and the slightly angled black eyes, and also the great good sense that prompted most of these youngsters to steer clear of gaudy purples and reds and choose dresses and shirts in clear yellows and white—colors that enhanced those beautiful coppery skins.

After the traffic rush in the hall subsided, classroom doors closed and bells rang. I found the principal's office. A pleasant young Indian woman presided over the standard golden oak desk with the standard green blotter and the standard wooden letter tray. I told her who I was and asked for Mr. Many Tall Trees.

"Mrs. Black, what kept you?" she asked. "Guy never stirred out of here his whole lunch hour."

I explained about the flat tire, and wondered again that she called the principal by his first name.

"He's in Mrs. Leonard's history class now," she told me. "It's last period. He'll be through in half an hour, and then he'll come back here. I've never seen that boy so eager about anything before."

The light began to dawn. "You mean Guy Many Tall Trees is a student here?" I said. I thought he was—"

"The principal?" she interrupted. "Hardly. In fact, he's in a small spot of trouble with the principal. He wrote to you on the school letterhead, didn't he, Mrs. Black?"

I nodded.

"Yes," she said. "Well, he's eager. He offered to help in the office, and he lifted the stationery. Not grand larceny, exactly, but the principal didn't appreciate it."

I could understand that. And I could also understand how Mr. Many Tall Trees, who would be happy to participate in the television program, had been able to intercept my letter. I guessed at that moment who the anonymous poet of Browning High was. He had baited the hook with that little verse and I had been reeled in right on schedule. I had to admire him. Also, if he wanted to be on "The Indispensables" that badly, I felt I had to talk with him. I could wait until three, but that was not really what I wanted to do.

"Could I go into the history class?" I asked the woman. It wasn't a bizarre request. School officials often turned me loose in classes. It was a good way to get to know the kids. They were on their own ground and they had their friends with them, so they didn't feel the need to shut me out.

The woman looked doubtful, but she got up and went through the door which was behind her desk. She was back in a minute or two with the genuine principal of Browning High—a gentleman named Mr. Nace. She had relayed my request to him, and he didn't object to the idea of my invading the history class. He led me out of the office and down the corridor and opened a classroom door.

The history class contained about thirty kids and one somewhat harried woman who must have been Mrs. Leonard. Mr. Nace introduced me and then hovered while I talked a little about "The Indispensables" and said we had had some mail from Browning. I didn't mention Guy Many Tall Trees right off, but I wondered aloud whether some of the Browning students might like to appear on the show.

A tall Indian boy in the back put up his hand. "How about three weeks from last weekend, Mrs. Black?" he asked.

"Perfect," I said. "Are you Guy Many Tall Trees?" I knew the answer to that one before I asked it.

He stood up and admitted it, and then sat down again. The other kids stared at him impassively. Not one of them volunteered a remark or a suggestion or showed any emotion whatever. This didn't surprise me. All kids are sensitive, and I knew that Indian kids, especially proud, were especially sensitive. It might well take a can opener to get anything out of this group—with the exception of Guy, of course.

I started on neutral ground. I talked about time and transportation. Then I edged over into what we might do on the show. I asked for suggestions.

Guy was first, and then one by one the other kids joined him. They talked about the culture of the Blackfeet. I was delighted to learn that they were still taught many of the old tribal beliefs, customs, and dances. They talked about how they got their names. When a baby was born, they said, the father walked out of the tepee or tent or house or hospital and looked around him, and he named the child after the first thing he saw. Thus we had Guy Many Tall Trees and Lorna Pool of Water.

"My old man walked out of the house and fell flat on his face," said one boy. The class laughed.

"What's your name?" I asked.

"Thomas Dirt in the Face," he said.

I asked for volunteers for the show and a lot of hands went up. Mr. Nace eliminated several of the kids for reasons best known to himself, but he could not have been too upset about the purloined letterhead. He did not give the axe to Guy Many Tall Trees. We decided on two panels with four kids to a panel. We also recruited six boys, two of whom would play tom-toms and four of whom would perform ritual dances. The rain dance and the love dance would be best, they decided.

It was long after three when I was ready to leave. Guy Many Tall Trees almost trampled three classmates getting to the front of the room so he could walk me to my car. I was just as pleased, since I was curious to know why he'd gone to so much trouble to pass himself off as principal. He told me that in a way it was true; he was student body president. Besides, he wanted the kids from Browning to be on "The Indispensables," and he was afraid I wouldn't pay any attention to a letter from a kid—a letter written on lined notebook paper.

"I paid attention to a poem written on lined notebook paper," I reminded him.

"Yeah. And then you wrote to the principal," he said.

"Well, why didn't you let the principal answer?" I asked. "After all, it *was* his letter."

Guy shrugged. "How could I be sure he'd say the right thing?"

He was wrong, of course. He'd acted like Secret Agent 17-X in a third rate movie. But he was marvelously effective. I drove home with the good feeling that we would have a pip of a show with the young redskins.

In the days that followed, I got several letters from Guy and other Browning High kids. They were excited, and Polly, Bud, Suzie, and the others were impressed by their enthusiasm. Somehow we all felt that the show would be an important step ahead for "The Indispensables," and we wanted it to be great for the group from Browning. We all got tense about it. I know I didn't sleep more than three hours the night before the show.

The school bus from Browning was due at the studio at two in the afternoon. We went on the air at four, and we figured we'd need the two hours to talk, have camera rehearsal for the dancers, and show the guests where to change clothes.

Our guests did not arrive at two, or at two-thirty, or at three.

By three-thirty our director was on the verge of a coronary. At quarter to four, Casey, our studio receptionist, opened the back door and waved at me. The Browning High bus was chugging up the hill. I grabbed George and Polly and we ran out.

Of all the people in the world, it was Mr. Nace, the principal, who was driving that bus. He didn't explain why he was so late; I didn't ask. I was so glad to see them as they piled off: Jean Up the South Side, Thomas Dirt in the Face, Lorna Pool of Water, Guy Many Tall Trees, a gaggle of others—and about ten dogs. All Indians have dogs, always.

Polly and George hurried the kids into the studio. Casey ran and got ropes and we anchored the dogs to the outside of the studio. The dogs protested loudly, but it didn't matter. The studio was soundproof. Casey and I came in and closed the doors.

I was telling the first four Indian kids where they would sit for the panel when we got the two-minute cue. Mark was suddenly beside me, all charm and hospitality, asking if he might seat the panelists. It was like Mark to want to get into the act—any act—but I was only grateful. I was getting desperate signals from the cameraman to get into position for the opening. I turned the kids over to Mark and heard him say, "Right this way. I have name cards all ready for you."

I had two minutes to open, welcome everyone, and give a rundown on the show. In addition to our panelists and the dancers, a bunch of the Browning kids had come to be in the audience. Polly had ushered them into two rows of seats down in front. They sat there and stared at me with that stony control that is characteristic of Indians. I kept telling myself that they were enthusiastic, happy, and excited; they had written and told us so.

George, always reliable, herded the drummers and the four dancers to the spot that had been lighted for the rain dance.

I introduced the dancers and the tom-toms thumped. The performance started slowly, then picked up and built and built. They were fantastic. The audience—their own from Browning and another hundred or so from Great Falls—never stirred until they finished.

As they danced, I moved over to the academic set to get ready for the first panel. There was Polly trying almost tearfully to get four Indian kids to sit down, and there were four Indian kids standing like statues. I couldn't see, at first, what the trouble was. Then I got a look at the name cards which Mark had so thoughtfully put on the table. We had a place for Pocahontas and one for Geronimo. Also Cochise and Sitting Bull.

Good old Mark. Hammy old Mark. He had the name cards all ready. And I had warned him that these kids were sensitive!

Polly and I did get them to sit down, but they had dried up. Mark had seen to that. They wouldn't talk even when we showed a film of their school. I found myself looking across at Polly and saying things like "How many students do you have at Browning High?" Polly, who had never been within ten miles of Browning High, gave answers like, "Ah . . . about fifteen hundred, aren't there?" If you can consider that an answer. The Indian kids didn't even nod, and when I asked Thomas Dirt in the Face about the above-average academic rating at Browning, Mark's voice floated through the studio. "They cheat a lot," said Mark.

Mark was such a help. What would we ever have done without him that day?

As Polly and I struggled through this panel, I could see Guy, Lorna Pool of Water, and the Indian dancers. They were in a corner of the studio, whispering fiercely. I also saw Mark. He was breaking up. He had never been so amused.

After two or three centuries, the time allotted for the panel was over and we went to a one-minute commercial. The love dance was to follow this. I staggered off the academic set and collided with Guy Many Tall Trees. "Can I be with you when you introduce the next dance?" he asked. "The guys want to change it to the war dance. It's more dramatic."

It was okay with me as long as they did some kind of dance. I had been afraid they wouldn't perform at all.

We got the cue and took our places for the introduction. I announced the dance and then asked Guy if he had something to say to the audience. "Yes," he said. "The war dance is our favorite. We'd like to have a student from 'The Indispensables' participate, if you don't mind."

There was a spatter of applause. Guy pointed toward Mark. "We'd like that one," he said.

Mark grinned. Any act at all, and he'd get in it if he could. "Great!" he said, and was among the Indian kids.

They formed a circle and shoved him into the middle of it. The lights were dimmed and the tom-toms began a slow, chilling beat. The dancers moved, crouching, around Mark. The tom-toms picked up the beat and the dancers moved faster, leaping. Mark watched them and began taking leaping little steps himself.

Each of the Indian boys carried a brightly painted stick with a feather fastened to one end. As the dance went on, they waved these sticks and uttered war cries. Show-off Mark yelped, too. There was a sudden roll from the tom-toms and one of the young braves tapped Mark on the shoulder with his feathered stick. It didn't hurt Mark, but it moved him out of the center of that human circle. He stopped grinning long enough to look surprised.

Another Indian boy tapped him. This time I heard a "whop!" Mark flew across the circle, and there was another "whop!"

"Hey you guys!" yelled Mark.

The feathered sticks went up and came down, went up and came down.

"Not so rough, Tonto!" protested Mark.

The feathered sticks moved and moved and Mark began to spin. They had him bounding around that circle so fast that he couldn't even drop to his knees and crawl out.

I began to be frightened. The mike was over the drums, so the audience couldn't hear Mark's cries. They sat spellbound as the drums beat louder and the war whoops grew shriller.

Then the dancers bent and closed in tight around Mark. I couldn't see him at all. The drums stopped. The whoops stopped. The young warriors froze, then stepped back away from Mark. Charming, indispensable Mark tried to take a step. He staggered, tripped over his own feet, and fell flat on his face. The Blackfeet did one turn around him and left him on the floor. He was almost in tears.

The audience cheered.

The Blackfeet had made their points. They left it to Bud to help Mark off. Guy and Lorna and two other kids took places on the academic set with George and me. I was watching the cameraman for the cue so I only had time to say to Guy, "Okay, he had it coming. Now give us a break, huh?"

Guy did. He talked. He talked about what it was like to be an Indian, to live a sheltered life on a reservation. He talked about the close family culture of the Blackfeet. "We're a minority group," he said, "but we're not like other minority groups. We haven't been taught that others might make fun of our culture, and so when that happens we don't know how to cope with it. We don't know how to fight the white man's way, or the black man's way."

"I'll put my money on you anytime," said George. His eyes went to the place where Mark had fallen. But Mark had not really been hurt. He was sitting over at the far side of the studio trying to shake his head clear. "Don't you think the word 'fight' is a little strong?" asked George.

"No," said Guy. "The Indian has had to fight ever since the white man came to this country, and he's been beaten so badly he has almost no fight left in him. That's our big problem."

"When my parents were young," said Lorna Pool of Water, "they went to college. They got degrees so they could get into government work and try to help their people. But it didn't work. So they came back to the reservation and raised children, and they raised their children just as they'd been raised. They lost their fight."

"Do you think that will happen to you?" I asked her.

"I could say no, but I don't know," she admitted. "When we came here today, we found a white boy who obviously doesn't like Indians. I saw him and I wanted to walk right out of here and go back to Browning. It's easier that way, but it's wrong."

"The Indian is hurt quickly and deeply," said Guy. "He doesn't get over his hurt. He broods."

Suzie and Bud, fascinated, had moved in very close to camera range. Guy saw them and pushed back his chair to make room for them. But there wasn't enough room at the table, so the Indian kids left the set and crouched in a circle on the floor. Suzie, Bud, Polly, George, and I could all be in on the discussion. The kids talked back and forth, and they found that they had lots in common. The working mother, who wants her children to have more material things, can be as big a problem among the Blackfeet as among the white kids of Great Falls. There's a generation gap on the reservation, too. The kids push for progress and the parents cling to tradition. In spite of this, we could see that these youngsters respected their parents. They respected their elders. Age commands respect.

Polly had to drag it out of him, because Guy was trying to be very polite to his white hosts, but he admitted that the Indian youngsters were often shocked and upset by the white kids who did not give due respect to adults.

I signaled the director to let the panel go on through the hour. We could skip the final musical number by our own rock group, which meant skipping Mark's big moment. But Mark had had enough big moments for one day.

When the panel was over, all fourteen of the Indian kids came on for the ending, and then the cameras were turned on the audience. They scanned along the two rows of Indian guests in front and the Great Falls kids clapped.

We were off the air, and someone opened the door to the outside world. We were assaulted by joyful barks. "Where'd these dogs come from?" yelled a voice. It sounded as if a man was being strangled.

I was not the first one out of the studio, since there were so many lively kids present. When I did get to the door the parking area outside was lathered with something frothy. A dog who might have been part Saint Bernard and part horse was sitting on a man and lapping something fuzzy and yummy off the main's face. The man was screaming for someone to get this monster off him. Casey, the receptionist, was hanging onto the door and laughing as if her head would fall off.

Casey filled me in on the details later. Mr. Orval Thorn, president of the Orval Thorn Bakery, had pulled up to the studio in one of his crispy-clean Orval Thorn Bakery trucks. He and his driver loaded their arms with whipped-cream pies and butter-frosted cakes and headed for the door, all set to begin work on the Orval Thorn commercials, starring Mr. Thorn. The studio shot these five at a time. Mr. Thorn and his driver were so taken up with their goody-good baked goods that they hadn't given thought to those friendly Indian dogs. Casey had heard the screams from her reception desk and had run out to see one of the station's best clients flat on his back and seriously beset by dogs.

The Indian kids hauled their dogs off and loaded them, slobbering whipped cream, aboard the bus. Casey went for towels for Mr. Thorn. Mr. Nace climbed behind the wheel of the bus and the Browning group went down the hills with the kids hanging out of the windows waving and the dogs hanging out of the windows barking.

A few days later, Mark received one of the painted, feathered sticks in the mail. There was a note attached to it—a single word, *Ynto*. I didn't know what it meant and neither did Mark. George said he thought it meant "Peace."

Guy wrote me a note:

> TV is improving
> And White Man is, too.
> Uncle Sam's still a louse
> But your show is a coup.

It was on ruled notebook paper, but I paid attention to it.

7

The Big People

We never convinced Ted, our first director on "The Indispensables," that it was possible to do a show like that. He
stuck with us, however, and managed to smooth out some of
our problems. He cut down on the blare of our rock combo, for
example, by having all the mikes moved to the other side of
the studio when Mark and his group were on. After a couple
of months, we reached a truce, and we'd sit in the empty
studio after a show to talk things over. This usually meant a
review of what had just gone wrong. I enjoyed the sessions,
though they may not have been useful. The same things seldom
went wrong twice in succession.

At the beginning of our second season, we got a new director. Three weeks later he had developed an ulcer. Ulcers are
endemic among technical directors, but he took warning. He
asked to be removed from the show and Ted came back as our
director. He was later replaced by a thirtyish gentleman who
soon showed symptons of heart trouble. He was removed from
the show and Ted bounced back into our lives. About that
time, the show got national recognition.

We were used to being recognized in Montana and parts of Canada, though we never got over being excited by it. National recognition was something else, and the adrenalin level went way up when I was asked to go back to Philadelphia. The producers of ten shows which were aired locally in various parts of the country were to appear before about a hundred major broadcasters. The idea was to present new local program concepts to the station owners or managers.

Stu Hoxworth was jubilant. "You'll take along the tape of that show you did three weeks ago," he decided.

I reread the invitation. "That is a one-hour tape," I reminded Stu. "What I'm supposed to have is a ten-minute pilot."

But we didn't have the facilities to do a pilot in Great Falls. Truth to tell, the appearance in Philadelphia was not uppermost in Stu's mind. What was uppermost was the fact that Philadelphia is close to New York, and there were people in New York that Stu wanted me to see. It was for them that I was to lug along that one-hour tape.

So I went to Philadelphia without a ten-minute pilot, and I talked about "The Indispensables" for ten minutes. Then there were twenty minutes of questions and answers. Half an hour. That was all each producer was allowed. I don't remember much about that half hour because I was so scared I was numb. It must have gone well, though. Many of the broadcasters talked to me when the regular program was over. I was asked to send something visual to stations all over the country. I dutifully wrote down names and addresses, and then I left the City of Brotherly Love and headed for New York with my one-hour tape.

In spite of the bad press it gets, New York is an exciting place, and often a friendly place. Manhattan taxi drivers always know how to get where you want to go, provided it isn't some bizarre address in Brooklyn. Elevator starters are kindly about directing you to the north bank of elevators because the south bank reaches only as high as the twenty-third floor. Receptionists can be frightening, but one must remember that they are there to keep people out as well as to let people in. They inhabit rooms filled with handsome furniture in decorator colors. The decorator colors were orange and black that year, and every reception room had a planter which sprouted plastic tropicals, guaranteed not to wilt. The receptionists did not wilt, either. They were fortified by lacquer and lip gloss. I suspect that some of them had been into the wonderful stuff that comes in small bottles and removes wrinkles—and stiffens up a face so that a smile is out of the question. The effect was of a series of manufactured ladies who might go "tick-tick-tick" if you got close enough to hear their inner workings.

I did not get that close. They never left the shelter of their dainty desks.

Secretaries in the inner offices were not so lacquered, and they were more harassed. Their inner workings seemed to be of genuine blood and bone and tissue and they all had a firm grasp on time—their bosses' time. With only so many hours in a day, they hoarded the minutes. They dealt out fifteen to one visitor and thirty to another. They held back telephone calls that weren't important and put through telephone calls that were. In between, they did everything from brewing coffee to filling out tax returns. I watched numbers of these girls operate while I waited for bosses; whatever a good secretary is paid, it probably is not enough.

Jolson DeWitt had a good secretary. I reached her after spending ten minutes with the plastic lady in the outer office. The secretary looked professionally distracted and was brewing coffee. She tucked me into a comfortable chair in her office and I waited while she put a telephone call from Lucille Ball through to Mr. DeWitt.

I had been five days in New York by the time I was steered from vice-president to vice-president and finally to Mr. DeWitt. I was tired. To a man, the vice-presidents had been interested. They had been downright enthusiastic about "The Indispensables." They thought it was a great concept. But I had learned one shattering truth during the five days. If "The Indispensables" went national, or was syndicated, it would mean the end of the good life in Great Falls. I wouldn't have time for the Sunday school class. I wouldn't have time for sessions with the kids when they gathered around the breakfast bar in the kitchen. I wouldn't have time for any of the things that make days delightful.

I wondered about Mr. DeWitt. What kind of man was he? Should I say no firmly and courteously right away, and not take up his valuable time?

The telephone call from Lucille Ball ended. The secretary, whose name was Miss Kaufman, opened the door to the inner sanctum and relieved me of my tape. "I'll give this to the projectionist," she told me.

I thanked her and stepped through the doorway to find myself mired ankle-deep in rust-colored carpeting. I blinked. Mr. DeWitt's office would have accommodated the Great Falls baseball team with room left over for the girls' field hockey finals. There was a gargantuan and most expensively simple desk and a conference table. Bookshelves climbed from floor to ceiling on one wall. Two other walls gleamed with the dark, restrained elegance of mahogany paneling. The fourth wall was pure window. One corner was infested with plastic, that ubiquitous wilt-proof greenery. Out of the ersatz jungle jutted a pedestal topped by a bust of John Barrymore.

Mr. DeWitt himself was out of scale in that room. He wasn't tall enough to hold his own against the huge desk. But he was not plastic. No one would ever purposely construct a person with such bloodshot eyes. He did not go "tick-tick-tick." He breathed in and out and he shook. I could feel it when he took my hand.

He was top drawer, however. At least everything that he had on had come out of the top drawer that morning. The suit was a proper gray—almost black—and sleek. The cufflinks were so massive that I wondered he could lift his hands. One did not think of Mr. DeWitt as wearing a shirt. He wore linen, and it was snowy.

"Sit down, dear lady," he said. I edged into an armchair facing the desk and discovered that I was also out of scale. When I tried to lean back my feet left the floor and stuck straight out. I felt like a kindergarten tot who had wandered into the eighth grade by mistake.

Mr. DeWitt sat down behind his desk and touched a button. Mrs. Kaufman's voice came through the intercom.

"Coffee, Miss Kaufman," ordered Mr. DeWitt. "Also aspirin. Four aspirins. And lots of coffee, black. And immediately, Miss Kaufman."

"Shall I hold all calls?" asked the secretary.

"Don't be an idi—ah, no, Miss Kaufman. That won't be necessary. This will be a rather short meeting, and I'm sure that Miss . . . ah . . ." He rustled some papers on the desk.

"Mrs. Black," I prompted.

"Yes, thank you. Mrs. Black and I won't be too long. But hurry with the coffee."

He pushed a second button and the intercom went dead.

"Slight headache," he explained. "Pressure. This is a pressure business."

There was a pipe rack on the desk, and he reached to select a pipe from it. He stuck the pipe between his teeth but did not light it. Instead he rummaged again through the stack of papers in front of him.

"Let's see now, you wanted to see me about . . ."

My heart ached for him. No one should have to talk to a lady television producer on such a morning—especially since the schedule of the day's appointments seemed to have gone astray.

"John Courtney suggested I see you," I explained, "but I really—"

"Ah, yes!" He smiled. He had come up with the scoop sheet. "Jane Black. Show called 'The Indispensables.' John talked to me about you." He was reading from the paper. "Just won national recognition with your little show, eh? Big youth image, John tells me. Unique concept."

He put down the paper and began to fill his pipe. "That vigorous teen generation is growing," he conceded. "Whether we like them or not, we can't ignore them, can we, Mrs. . . . Mrs. . . ."

"Black."

"Yes. Mrs. Black."

He picked up the paper again and mumbled through it. "Proven concept . . . good image . . . five commendations, ease, candor . . . certain sophistication . . . music and . . . GREAT FALLS, MONTANA!"

He put down the paper and looked across at me. "Calamity Jane has descended upon us!" he exclaimed.

I felt very, very tired. I didn't answer.

"You mean they've got local television stations out on the great western plains?"

"Two channels," I said, not very nicely.

He began to tap the stem of his pipe against his even, white teeth. "John didn't tell me you came into town by horse and wagon," he grinned. "Trail a bit rough?"

I tried to wriggle out of that huge chair, but he waved me back. "Now ma'am," he said, "you've got to remember that this is New York. This is the big city. Why, do you know there

are more people right here in this building than in the whole
state of Wyoming?"

"Montana," I corrected him, "and this isn't my first time in
New York. I can . . ."

Miss Kaufman glided in with a tray. She had coffee, two
cups, and a neat little shot glass with four aspirins. She poured,
handed the cups and glided out, leaving Mr. DeWitt to his
aspirins and his little jokes.

"Tell me," he said, "do they have real see-ment sidewalks
in Wilting Springs or are they still using the old wooden ones?"

I wanted to tell him that we paved our streets with gold
nuggets but I was afraid that if I opened my mouth I would
cry.

He busied himself washing down aspirins with coffee. I
sipped and washed down that lump in my throat and reflected
that he probably lived in a small world. If he had ever been
west of Princeton he wasn't letting on.

He started going through the scoop sheet again. To give
myself something to do, I opened my purse and took out my
reading glasses and put them on. It helped. Jolson DeWitt
became an indistinct shape behind the desk.

I thought about John Courtney, the man who had so kindly
and so sincerely encouraged me to set up this appointment with
DeWitt. John was a born New Yorker, and certainly as successful as this man. How could he have been so wrong? "Jolson
should see your show," he had said. "That's Jolson's business—
to recognize an attractive approach to what's vital today. The
whole country is looking for that wholesome quality. Jolson
will see this."

Jolson did see the show. Without further quips, he pushed
one of the buttons on his intercom. "Jimmy," he said into
the box, "are you ready to roll the tape that came in this
morning? It's called 'The Indispensables.' "

"Ready when you are, Mr. DeWitt," said a male voice.

"Then go ahead," said DeWitt. "But hold the volume down, will you?"

"Right, Mr. DeWitt."

Drapes which must have been controlled from the projection room slid across the big windowed wall. The lights went out and a panel opened to show a screen in one of the mahogany walls. The snappy, swinging musical theme of "The Indispensables" filled the office.

I slid around in the big chair so I could watch, and I had a sudden surge of confidence. In a few minutes, and with a few barbed words, this man had made me feel like Little Bo Peep hawking cotton candy at a cocktail party. Now I saw the kids on the screen, performing with their wonderful, wide-eyed candor, and I felt real pride.

It was a good show. It was our best. We had had eight teen-agers belting out a professional rendition of "When the Saints Go Marching In." We had had a panel of four high-school students talking about the moral issue of the Vietnam War.

Mr. DeWitt got from behind his desk and moved in the darkness to a chair near mine. He sat down, leaned back, and was very quiet. I felt myself warm again. In spite of his caustic manner, DeWitt must have been impressed by the kids. They were smooth, acute, intelligent.

The show went on and I forgot about DeWitt. There was more music and there was the sports segment with film clips of a high-school track star breaking records at the national level. This was followed by a smoothly paced interview.

When the show was nearly over, the spell was broken. A horrible, horrible sound rumbled through the office.

Jolson DeWitt was snoring!

I got up and went to the desk. I found the right button in the dark and pressed it. "Jimmy?" I said.

"Yes?" The voice came through, puzzled.

"Please rewind that tape immediately and send it in to Miss Kaufman. I'm leaving."

Jimmy didn't answer, but in a moment the screen went black and the mahogany panel closed and the drapes slid open. Jolson DeWitt blinked awake.

I didn't say anything.

He hauled himself up and rubbed his face and had the grace to apologize. The tendency to catnap was, he said, one of the unfortunate symptoms of those dreadful middle years which were almost upon him. He buzzed Miss Kaufman and ordered more coffee. Then he explained that he had two teen-age children of his own. They were being educated abroad. Neither he nor his wife could cope with their hostile attitudes. "Impossible," was the word he actually used.

He took my hand and held it. "You have courage, dear lady," he said. I wished he'd stop calling me dear lady. I knew it was only because he couldn't remember my name, but it made me feel like something out of Tennyson. "You have real courage. You must be the Joan of Arc of Wyoming."

"Montana."

"Yes, Montana. Now let me give you a bit of advice, and I hope you'll think of it often. Take your little show back to Wilting Springs and be proud of it, but forget your dreams of glory. Pardon my brutal frankness, but please do not try to bring that cornball concept down out of the hills. You'd only make yourself a laughing stock."

He stepped to the window and gestured toward the concrete and steel and glass towers around us. "These are big people here," he told me. "They think big."

Again he took my hand. "I'm sure you're pleased that I am being completely honest with you," he said.

I did not feel like crying any more. I felt like doing something violent and physical. "I am pleased," I told him. "I am so pleased that I'd better get out of here before I get emotional about it."

I pulled away and got to the door. Miss Kaufman had my tape ready. I seized it and fled out past the plastic plants and the plastic receptionist and down to the street, where I found a taxi.

Why did I care? I didn't want to be big people anyway. But I was mad—so mad that when I got to the hotel I jammed the zipper in the back of my dress and an amused floor maid had to rescue me. I caught the late flight back to my western plateau and my cornball teen-agers and my little people, and to this day I cannot abide planters filled with plastic tropicals.

8

The Valley of the Sun

If you get really wrapped up in it, a hobby can become a profession. Perhaps it would not have happened to me if we had stayed in Great Falls. In Great Falls, "The Indispensables" was pure and simple hobby. It was fun. I loved the kids. I loved lugging props around in the car and visiting the schools and all those other nice things.

We didn't stay in Great Falls, however. My family moved to Phoenix. We had had property there for years. We'd talked about making the move for years. Finally, in 1966, we pulled up stakes and headed south.

I can remember Jack's comment as we drove into the city. It was one word. "Keen!"

It was keen. Phoenix isn't beautiful the way Paris is beautiful, or San Francisco, or Rome. It isn't romantic. But it is clean and stark and new and bright. It's desert with palm trees. It's cactus gardens next to flower gardens. It's gleaming buildings flung out like dice on the valley floor and weird red rocks erupting in improbable places to show off their wind carvings.

Phoenix is also big. There were more than a million people in the Valley of the Sun. We had had four high schools in

Great Falls. Today, after more than four years, I am never sure exactly how many there are in the valley. Lots. Plus Arizona State University and several colleges.

Well, I thought, good. The more schools, the more kids. The more kids, the more Indispensables. I can keep on having fun. I paved the way with a telephone call, and then hurried over to meet the president of the NBC affiliate station. His name was Dick Lewis and he was a delight. By a weird coincidence he was just back from a managers' meeting in Hawaii and he had heard about "The Indispensables" from some of the New York network people.

Mr. Lewis, however, was not Stu Hoxworth. Things could not be decided in Phoenix as quickly as in Great Falls. It was just plain too big. A show like "The Indispensables" could be involved—and expensive.

So began the meetings. There were meetings with advertising directors and meetings with program directors and meetings with sales directors. There were meetings where everybody talked and no one listened. There were meetings which I recall only as faces blurring into faces. And there were the meetings where you could quickly tell where the power was. It was with the man who didn't need to watch any of the others because all the others were watching him, and trying to read

Then there was the meeting with Sherman Payne, who handled the advertising for Arizona Public Service. That will stand out in my mind forever.

Sherman Payne had his problems with me before we even met. He had to be a telephone touring service. The administrative offices of APS are in an especially jumbled area of downtown Phoenix. When I called for an appointment, I got the most detailed and meticulous instructions on how to get from our place to Mr. Payne's office. I wrote everything down carefully and read it back to Mr. Payne. Then, to be utterly, completely safe, I took along my city map and allowed myself an extra half hour for the drive.

I might have been on time were it not for the railroad tracks. Railroad tracks disorient me, especially when they cross a street on the diagonal. I bumped over two sets of rails and zigged when I should have zagged and was in a cul-de-sac where men were loading crates aboard trucks. I backed out of that one and went around the block to begin again. The block ended up someplace where I had no business to be. A nice gas station man advised me to go down an alley and turn left and start at the railroad tracks again, and when I tried that I found a different hunk of tracks. I located a pay telephone and called Mr. Payne and said I was on my way and got more instructions. Then I got tangled up with more railroad tracks.

I wanted to drive the car onto the right of way and follow the steel rails out of town and nevermore return. I resisted the temptation and finally made it to APS. I was more than an hour late and my dress was sticking to my back in the 113-degree heat.

"Everybody gets lost coming here," said Mr. Payne. He was a tall, calm soul, slender, with brown hair nicely graying at the temples. He had a very efficient water cooler, which I did appreciate, and a big office with a big desk and a big chair, and he was in scale. He could stand up to it. Or sit down in it.

He also had four children, two of whom were in their teens, and he was both mournful and excited about youth.

"You remember that boy in Tucson?" he asked me.

I remembered. The case had been in headlines about a year before. The boy had murdered several teen-age girls in a particularly horrendous fashion. Mr. Payne wondered, as we all did, why. He also wondered why the 98 percent of the kids who do not commit murder or hold up candy stores are ignored. We talked for three hours about kids, and about the fact that they are different today—and most are bright and sharp and good. He wanted to do something about those bright, sharp, good kids, and he was eager about "The Indispensables."

But we would have to do a pilot. That was plain from the start. That was the way it was done in larger markets. The program directors and sales managers worked with a real visual, not a verbal concept. Sherman Payne would have to convince his company. Everyone needed to see an actual production.

I went home and brooded. I had to do a pilot, and I didn't have the kids. The schools weren't in session. Principals and advisers weren't on tap.

"Charlie must know some kids," said Jack.

"Charlie?" I said.

"Charlie Jennings. You remember the Jennings. They used to live in Great Falls and they moved to Scottsdale last year. I called Charlie while you were out and he said we should come over this afternoon."

I didn't even stop to check out the invitation with Charlie's mother. I took a shower, put on a fresh dress, and we drove out to Scottsdale.

The Jennings were ready and waiting and welcoming. They had lemonade and advice, a patio and a pool, and Charlie had several school yearbooks. We went through them. Charlie made telephone calls and young people started to arrive. It took some time and a lot of talk, but we found a boy and a girl to host the show, a pair to do the Triple-T segment, and two top golfers who had film on their winning rounds in the spring tourney. Charlie was also in touch with a bunch of boys who had formed a combo. He assured me that they sounded exactly like the Tijuana Brass, and he was right. Charlie even offered to be part of a panel to discuss the great thing called the generation gap.

It was Jack, though, who suggested the slight change in the format of the show. "Do you really need an adult host?" he said. "Why not have all teen-agers?"

I hesitated. I had never thought of such a thing. On the other hand, why not? It could make for a stronger youth image.

"You know, kids are sharper now than you used to be when you were young, Mom," Jack said quickly.

"How would you know?" I asked him. "You weren't around when I was young."

But he was right. He was only saying what Sherman Payne had said. The new generation had been exposed to more. They wanted to do more on their own. They were more articulate. They were also demanding, opinionated, sometimes infuriating, and almost always interesting.

"We'll try it," I decided. "It may not work, but we can try it."

We had a week to get ready for the pilot. We were still pretty much at sixes and sevens in our house, with furniture standing tentatively where the movers had put it down. The Jennings offered the use of their beautiful, big home for rehearsals and we began to whip things into shape.

among the new Indispensable hosts, as well as in the combo, and we decided to throw in a cast number. We had done cast numbers often and successfully in Great Falls. The hosts would let their hair down and work out a wildly swinging version of the hottest novelty pop song going. It always brought the house down.

The big hit in the summer of 1966 was a song called "Little Red Riding Hood." It was a rock version that had Little Red running through the woods, pursued by a two-legged wolf. The Jennings were most thoughtful about the woods. They had too many trees in their yard anyway, said Mrs. Jennings. They did some quick pruning, and we had branches enough for a reasonable forest.

The great day arrived. We were to tape the pilot at the studio, and I arrived loaded with props. Just like Great Falls,

I thought. I had a wolf's head. I had a red flannel hood for Little Red. I had the tree limbs from the Jennings' yard.

Naturally, I had met the director. He was a delightful young man who loved the idea of doing a pilot with kids. The rest of the crew were delightful older men who thought I was a phoney at best, and might also be violently insane.

The director ignored the grumbles and mutterings of the crew and got busy making one area of the studio look like a woods. We had an area set up for the combo and another for the academic set, which we would also use for the sports set. We had two brightly painted stools for the Triple-T kids. We had two letters saved from Great Falls to be used on the Triple-T segment.

We got through the pilot beautifully. I couldn't believe the finished product when I saw it. I was in awe of the equipment. I had loved our little station in Great Falls, but this was superior technically. The young people gave it their all. Our host made an admirable wolf, lumbering through the woods after Sherry, the hostess, who was a toothsome Little Red in that flannel hood. I was so happy with the hosts and the combo that I asked them then and there if they'd be permanent Indispensables if the show went on the air. They would. They were so excited. And I drove home in a state of euphoria.

Then the waiting began. I waited for a month before I knew. I waited and I fielded telephone calls from the would-be Indispensables. When they didn't call, the kids dropped in to visit. They talked about what happened yesterday or this morning. Then they asked if I had heard whether the show would go or not. And then they always talked about the kind of panels they would like to have, and as they talked the gripes began to come out. Some of them weren't happy with the school administrations. None of them liked the idea of the war in Vietnam. Phoenix was beginning to have a smog problem. No one used the word *ecology* but they talked plenty about pollution. They gave me all kinds of ideas. I made scads of notes. And I began to be troubled. The generation gap I knew. We certainly had had it in Great Falls. We had wrestled with it in every Sunday school class. We had hashed it out on television panels. Yet, in some way, all the talk that first summer in Phoenix was slightly different. I think I felt a stirring of rebellion—real rebellion. I had a sense of things boiling very near the surface.

I decided it was going to be an interesting season, if we had a season. Then the word came. "The Indispensables" *would* have a season in Phoenix, and we had a week to get ready. And we were on.

Sherman Payne was like a godfather to us. He did everything to help. He did things no one else would have thought about, such as arranging a slush fund for me. I was to have fifteen dollars a week to buy cokes and hamburgers for the kids whenever it seemed appropriate. He even set up an office for me at APS, down there among the railroad tracks. Every day he or his artists or his promotion people would come in with some exciting new suggestion on what could be done to promote the show. And one day I looked out to see a city bus go past emblazoned with a sign: WATCH THE INDISPENSABLES. We'd never been on a city bus before!

The director who had done the pilot with us went on vacation just after our first show. We got a new director—a brilliant but fierce young man named Ray DeTourney. If there can be such a thing as a creative, efficient tornado, Ray was one. He wanted the Indispensables to be pros. He wanted network quality. He glowered at us from the control room while smoking huge black cigars, and he flew out in clouds of nicotine to rattle us up when we did things wrong. We were taping, not doing a live show, so when we did things wrong we could do them over right. When we got to know Ray better we realized that one of the fiercest things about this involved young genius was his ever-present cigar.

We had our own permanent set in that dream of a studio, with "The Indispensables" spelled out in dancing, six-foot letters. The "Romper Room" lady had a separate studio, so we could all sit down without fear. Also, as the weather got cooler, we were up to our ears in celebrities. We had had three big names on "The Indispensables" in Great Falls. In Phoenix, we had them all the time. They came for the golf or to relax in the Valley of the Sun or for appearances at one of our many theaters or simply because they liked Phoenix. Hugh Downs was to move to Carefree, Arizona, a new Shangri-La outside of town, and he became one of our favorite guests. John Davidson came and spent much more than the allotted interview time with the kids, and they loved him. Dick Van Dyke, who had once been a disc jockey in Phoenix, came back with a schedule as tight as the countdown for a space launching, but he squeezed us in and gave us a filmed interview. We got exclusive interviews with Peggy Fleming and Bobby Goldsboro. Sometimes these stars sat in on our panels—and the panels were becoming more and more provocative and more and more controversial. Many times they stirred up the adults. They distressed the adults. They made the adults think about things they didn't want to think about.

Soon the word *Indispensables* was being mentioned all over the valley. The signs on the busses helped. So did signs that went up on benches throughout the city. Perhaps some of the people didn't know what Indispensables were, but they knew Indispensables existed, and they were curious. Also, we were having from forty to a hundred student guests a month—guests for sports, for panels, for music. Every time a student appeared, everybody in his school suddenly tuned in to "The Indispensables."

It was all grand, grand, grand. But it wasn't a hobby anymore. It was a profession.

9

Pills, Pot, and Parents

At one party in Great Falls, I met a daddy who had solved the entire problem of the teen-ager. When he is thirteen, or perhaps twelve-and-a-half, you lock the kid in a closet. You do not let him out again until his twenty-first birthday. You insert a straw through the keyhole and feed him by pouring nourishing liquids through this.

Because of the Humane Society and other nosey institutions, that daddy never got to test this theory. The idea is intriguing, though, because the teen years are rough on parents. Not dull. Never dull. But rough.

For one thing, teen-age kids are seldom happy with their choice of parents. For another, they suddenly start talking a different language.

I was visiting friends one night when fifteen-year-old Martie announced to her father that she'd had a "bummer" that day.

"That's nice," he said. He was trying to listen to a newscast. Martie said something not at all nice and slammed upstairs.

"*Now* what's with her?" said the bewildered father.

"She told you," I said. "Didn't you listen?"

"Well sure," he said. He hadn't listened. "I just don't understand a word she says these days."

That figured. Because the word *bummer* should have brought that solid citizen to attention. It is one of those words. A bummer can be a bad day, which was what Martie had had. But a bummer could also be a bad trip, and not just over to Scottsdale. Good old Timothy Leary was preaching his gospel of mind expansion the first year we were in Phoenix; pot was big and LSD was big. There were youngsters, like good old Timothy, who could break your heart. And there were these words.

I never got used to it. I still can't get used to it. In Great Falls a few of the leather-jacket kids had fooled around with drugs. Everyone knew who they were, and the other kids cut them dead. I suppose the drug thing finally did hit Great Falls, but it was already in full swing in Phoenix when we got there, and there were the words. Bummer. Mary Jane. Acid. Speed. And they changed. They changed every month. They changed every week. They are still changing. Is "system" a thing devised by Bell Telephone? Not at all, not at all. Now a kid who is arrested for using narcotics is "in the system."

Of course we did a panel on LSD right off. The town was very uptight about it. It was a hot subject. The panel went very well. We had done our homework. I had gone to three psychiatrists to find out everything I could about the stuff, and I had reams of material for the moderator on the show. We'd found four high-school kids who had done papers on LSD and who had actually been with other kids when they were under the influence. They gave it both barrels.

Which was great, I thought. And then we began to get letters. Most of the audience who wrote in also thought the show was fine, but not all. "You only showed one side," wrote one girl. "You only showed the bad side, and that's not fair." Moreover, she signed her name.

There were a few others like this. There weren't enough to panic us, but there were enough to make me uneasy. There were some telephone calls, too. And then I had a chat with a boy we'll call Chuck. I knew him. He hung around the "Indispensables" set a lot. Many kids hung around the "Indispensables" set. They helped out any way they could. I suppose part of it was a show-biz thing; they wanted to be on the inside. And part of it was that it was a keen way to meet pretty girls. Boys like pretty girls, and that is one of the nicer basic facts of life. Let us pray that it does not change.

But Chuck did not have pretty girls on his mind the day he nailed me in the hall and practically backed me up against the wall. "Don't you think that was kind of a goody-goody panel?" he asked.

I hoped he didn't mean what I was afraid he meant. "The LSD thing?" I asked.

He meant the LSD thing. He went on and talked about the fantastically wonderful things LSD did for the mind, and he quoted Timothy Leary.

I didn't know what to say. I couldn't believe it. This was no hippie kid. He looked like a shorter, younger, blonder version of Jack Kennedy.

He went away, eventually, but a few days later he called me. I was invited to attend an LSD party.

"Not on your life," I said.

He didn't push it then, but he called again the next day. "Change your mind?" he asked. "You ought to come. You claim 'The Indispensables' is a show where kids can say their own thing, but that LSD panel was stacked."

In a way it was true. It had never entered my head to scour the valley for kids who thought LSD was the greatest thing since mother's milk. There had been some bad trips that had made the papers. I reminded Chuck of these, but he had the stock answer. Kids who couldn't handle LSD weren't stable to begin with; if the drug hadn't triggered their problems, something else would have.

"You're taking a big chance, you know," I told him. "I could turn you in."

"You won't," he said. "You're no fink. And if you haven't tried it, don't knock it."

"No way," I told him. "I'm a devout coward."

I hung up, but he called back and he dared and challenged and I finally agreed that I'd go. "But get this," I told him. "I will not eat, drink or smoke *anything* while I'm in that house."

"That's your loss," said Chuck. "But it'll be interesting."

It was. In its way, it was a memorable evening.

The address Chuck had given me was in the best part of town. The house was a big, solid Spanish colonial that rambled this way and that, and flung its gardens over more than an acre of expensive real estate. There was a curved drive in front, where I parked and brooded. Aside from a dim, orange bulb that burned in a wrought iron fixture near the door, I couldn't see a light. What if there was no one home? What if it was some stupid joke? Worse yet, what if it wasn't a joke? Was Chuck waiting for me in that big, dark house? If he was, who was with him? What were they doing?

I pulled myself together and went up the flagstone path. The door was massive and carved. I touched the bell and heard chimes. I waited. Nothing happened for a long time. I was about to turn and go away as quietly as I had come when the door swung open. I looked past a sturdy Spanish woman into a red-tiled foyer. The woman said nothing; she stood holding onto the door.

"Is Chuck in?" I asked.

She shrugged. I could have kicked myself. I hadn't taken

the trouble to find out Chuck's last name. He'd always been
around and he'd just been Chuck.

"Is the lady of the house in?" I asked. That inane question
would have warmed the heart of an Avon lady. It did not get
through to the Spanish woman. She shrugged again.

"Isn't anyone home?" By this time I was snappish.

The woman heaved herself away from the door and motioned
me in. As I passed her I realized that we had more than a
simple lack of communication. She was bombed. Somewhere in
that elegant house there was a wine jug and it wasn't full.

The woman took my arm and started propelling me through
rooms. I had been wrong; there were lights in the house, but
they were dim and the drapes were drawn. We went through
rooms covered with lush shag carpeting and across a patio or
two and even through a bedroom. We went up three steps here
and down two steps there and thirty seconds away from the
door I knew I was lost. You cannot get lost in someone's home,
unless it happens to be Buckingham Palace, but I was lost.

At last we came to a room that was simpler than the others.
It was rather like our family room back in Great Falls. My
guide shoved me through the doorway and left me, and I saw
Chuck. About a dozen other kids were sitting around listening
to the stereo. Except that it was a little too quiet, it looked
like a teen party anywhere, with the girls in their jeans and
bright shirts, the boys long-haired but neat. If they'd been
drinking Pepsi you could have photographed them for an ad.
They weren't drinking Pepsi, however. They weren't doing
much of anything, and there was a heavy odor in the room. I
hadn't encountered that before, but I could guess what it was.
Pot. So it wasn't just an LSD party. They were mixing things.

Chuck seemed pleased to see me. He explained that it wasn't
his house, and he introduced me to my hostess. She was a
petite and stunning blonde named Tarri. I met the other kids,

all of whom were nice and respectful. I saw no one take a pill or a sugar cube or anything else. I saw no one smoke anything. Out of deference for their square guest, they must have done their thing early—perhaps while I was sitting and brooding in the driveway.

Chuck had appointed himself vice-president in charge of filling me in on the scene. He was proud of the group, and when I asked him if Tarri's parents were at home, he looked at me as if I had lost my mind.

"Do you have kids?" he asked.

I told him I had three.

"Well, do you hang around when they have a party?"

"As a matter of fact, I do."

He laughed. "Archaic. Don't you know how uptight that gets them? It's like saying 'I don't trust you, baby.' Know what I mean, Little Mama?"

I looked around at that too-quiet bunch of kids. "I know what you mean," I told him.

He didn't get the point. He started in on the problems his generation had inherited. To listen to him, you'd think his parents had sat up late nights and gotten up early morning so they'd have extra time to construct these problems. I was getting Basic Lesson One: Kids who do weirdo things justify themselves, and they usually do it by blaming their parents. Parents are handy that way.

Basic Lesson Two followed. According to Chuck, the world is in such a ghastly mess that you have to expand your mind even to think about it. LSD is the thing to take for larger minds.

A few of the others joined us long enough to agree. With LSD you got the big picture. You saw things and thought thoughts you couldn't possibly manage any other way.

"Then what do you do?" I asked.

Nobody seemed to hear that one. I let it go. They didn't do anything and they wouldn't do anything. It was too easy to sit in that cool, comfortable room and see big things and think expanded thoughts.

Suddenly it wasn't comfortable, because the pretty blonde named Tarri pointed to the coffee table and made a throaty noise.

I looked at the coffee table. We all looked at the coffee table. There was nothing on it but one clean ashtray and a china figurine.

"That's it! It's coming!" cried Tarri.

The ashtray and the figurine stayed put, as good ashtrays and figurines have a habit of doing.

Tarri's voice shot up an octave. "Look! Look! It's growing! It's the alien. It will wipe out all the evil in the world!" She began to whimper.

I glanced at the others. I wanted to say, "Now see what you've done!" But they were staring at the figurine. Some of the girls squealed; one of the boys moaned. One cringed back and yelled that he didn't want to see it, but he kept staring. A couple held on to each other and shook.

"Listen to those tubas!" yelled Chuck. He was having his own private thing. He was wired into the stereo. I listened as well as I could to the music. Almost straight strings. No tubas. "What a crescendo!" said Chuck. "It's terrifying. Man, it really shakes me. Isn't it great?"

A small cat padded into the room. It was a fluffy little creature, only lately a kitten. It may have been drawn by curiosity, or by the desire for a nice pat on the head.

One of the girls focused—if you can use the word—on that cat. He was a jungle monster. Tiger, tiger burning bright! In fact he was two jungle monsters and they were going to eat each other up!

The little cat had no ambitions to star in this production. He humped his back, spit, and flew out of the room. I flew right after him.

I wanted to get hold of an adult—any adult. I skidded through the house looking for the Spanish maid. I could hear the cries from the family room as I stumbled through my search. Perhaps there were both good trips and bad trips going on in that room. They were very noisy trips, whatever the variety.

The maid had passed out on a bed. I don't know why I looked for her in the first place. She couldn't have helped.

There was more bumbling before I found the front door and shot out into the night. There was a light on in a house down the road. I ran. The man who answered the bell was in a sports shirt and slacks and his bare feet. I think he must have been in bed and then gotten up. His wife was huddled behind him in a robe and she was twisting her hands. Not all neighbors who watch and listen are nosey. Some of them care. These did.

"Do you know where the parents are—those parents—the house over there?" I pointed. He understood.

"It wouldn't do any good, lady," he told me. "We tried." He looked very anxious. "Sometimes it's worse. Sometimes there's a big crowd of them."

"I'm afraid they're going out of their minds," I told him.

We stood in that hallway and talked and worried and fussed. Neighbors have a natural aversion to calling the police about other neighbors. It's a thing they hate to do. But somebody had to get those kids down off cloud nineteen. The man did, finally, call the police.

That raid did not make the papers. No drugs were found in the house. But the kids were obviously freaked out, and the various parents were located. They had to go down to the police station. Police are funny about things like that. They don't send the kids home in a cab, and they ask awkward questions such as, "Well, where *were* you?" and "Why weren't you there?" and "Why didn't you know where she was?"

The parents protected their kids as best they could. They said there had never been drugs before. They probably meant it, too. How would they know? They weren't there. They probably didn't listen. Any one of those kids could have said, using the current term for the drug, "I'm going to an LSD party tonight," and the parents wouldn't have understood unless, by great attention and mental application, they had taken the trouble to learn the lingo.

Chuck called me two days after the party. He barely remembered that I had been there, and he didn't connect me with the raid. Or maybe he did; he stopped hanging around the "Indispensables" set. The kids had gotten off lightly and no one had been booked, but Chuck was thoroughly shaken up.

I heard no more from Chuck for several months, then he called again to tell me that Tarri, that lovely little girl, had been taken to a private mental hospital. Another boy who had been at the party that night had continued tripping, and he was in the hospital, too. Chuck didn't quote Timothy Leary on that call; he told me he was leaving the valley, but he promised to keep in touch. He did, too. I got calls on strange occasions and at strange times. One Christmas Eve he called from San Francisco. He wasn't on LSD; he was on pot, and he said he was celebrating "the birth of drugs" instead of that birth the rest of us poor sheep were celebrating.

It is almost four years later, and Chuck is back in Phoenix. He is not lounging around in any of the big houses in the best parts of town. He is in a shabby but immaculate little house on a short little street, together with about twenty other young men who have been the drug route. They are from here, there, and everywhere. They call their place the Inn of Love and they carry Bibles around with them. At Christmas they don't celebrate the birth of drugs because they know all about drugs. They don't celebrate much at all. They roam the valley trying to help kids who are hooked. Each of them, somehow, some way, has gotten clean and stayed clean. They say it's because of a power they didn't have themselves. I did an interview with them on "The Indispensables" and we had over a thousand calls on it. Kids who were on drugs called. Parents of hooked kids called. Kids who were tempted called.

LSD is not as big as it was because TV and magazines and newspapers have done a tremendous job with it. It is, however, still with us. Users who have had good trips keep on tripping; they don't believe they'll have a bad trip until it happens. Other drugs are dangerous, too. Speed can kill you. There are signs everywhere warning about this, but some kids still use speed. In New York there is a heroin epidemic. In Los Angeles one of the biggest problems is barbiturates—reds, downers. These are for the kids who really want to stop the world. They want to get off, and if they mix their reds with wine or beer they sometimes succeed. And there is pot everywhere. There is still the need to know the terms, to keep the lines of communication open, and this is not easy once a kid hits the teens and the hormone level starts bubbling up.

At thirteen, the little girl who once sat on Daddy's lap and thought he was a knight in shining armor may notice that Daddy is developing a small paunch and his forehead is getting too high. Also, Mom doesn't look like Barbara Stanwyck and she's tired a lot of the time. The teen-age boy does not want to go tadpole hunting with Dad any more, and the teen-age girl thinks father-daughter dinners are gruesome. So Mom and Dad lose their cool and scream, "I don't understand you any more!" And Sonny and Sis scream back, "You never did," or "You'd understand me if I were a broker's report," and the iron curtain slams down.

Visiting at Cathy's one day, I saw Cathy head for the door with steadfast purpose. Something important was happening elsewhere and she was not about to miss it.

"Where are you going now?" asked Cathy's mother.

Cathy pulled up short, looking slightly irritated. But her mother had a right to know. "Down to Slaboves to dig Ultra Sonic Gresham's Theorem," said Cathy, and she disappeared.

"Sound's orgiastic," said Cathy's mother, who sometimes uses words like that.

"It's a rock group," I told her. "I had them on 'The Indispensables.'"

"Oh," said Cathy's mother. She could have dropped it there, but when Cathy came back quite a while later she asked how Ultra Sonic Gresham's Theorem had been.

"Kee-ool!" said Cathy. "All the guys really throbbed with them." Cathy then sat down and talked at length about Ultra Sonic Gresham's Theorem and other things. She used many words we understood and a few we'd never heard before but could figure out taking them in context. We had to listen with care, though.

"I'm going to write a dictionary," said Cathy's mother, after Cathy had gone to bed.

"Forget it," I advised. "It would be out of date before they could set the type."

Which was true, but not important. What was important was that Cathy's mother had kept the iron curtain from closing. She and Cathy were talking, and listening.

Cathy went away for her first year of college where she really ran head-on into pot. Not that there hadn't been plenty of it in Phoenix, but at college she was living with it. Cathy's roommates used it, and some of the girls down the hall and lots of others. It was the thing to do.

I don't know how many kids would do what Cathy did, but when she began to consider marijuana, she called her mother. She was very casual, because nothing can be a big thing. "I'm thinking of trying pot," she said.

Her mother experienced that surge of adrenalin which signals real terror. She said quickly, "Why?"

Cathy had reasons. It didn't really hurt you. The other girls were doing it. And even if it was illegal, who would raid a girls' dorm?

Cathy's mother asked her to think about it some more. Then she sat up half the night writing and rewriting a letter. Cathy gave me a copy of it when she got home for the summer. It read in part:

> When I started smoking, Cathy, I was your age. It was the smart, sophisticated thing to do. It helped make me one of the "in" crowd. There was nothing wrong with it; all the really "sharp" people did it, and that was the image I wanted for me. Now I can't quit! At best, I can look forward to a shorter life. Or I can expect emphysema to make my final years a misery. Or, most dreadful of all—cancer! I know you'd do most anything if I could stop, but I can't. I depend on my cigarettes. Twenty-two years ago, smoking was harmless, medically. What will the medical opinion be tomorrow or next year or twenty years from now if you try—like—learn to depend on marijuana? I don't know. But, once hooked, all the medical advice in the world—even the fear of death—can't unhook you. Ask me. I know. At least about cigarettes.

And then the law! Should we flout law because it isn't perfect? Perhaps we have used the law to subjugate some, but think of the many who are free. Should we work within the law to effect changes needed, or destroy the instrument that makes ordered change possible? If enough disobey because they aren't in danger of being caught, then we will destroy all law.

Cathy hasn't tried marijuana. Her friends are still smoking it, and a couple of them are pushing, but it's still no big thing. They're not hooked. Cathy can look you calmly in the face and say they're not hooked.

But Cathy could also call her mother and say that one simple sentence, and her mother could ask that one simple question. Why?

That *why* might be the only thing that works. Maybe it would work even after the awful thing happens and your kid has been caught in a raid and you've had to make that terrible, humiliating visit to the police station.

"Why?"

Not, "Why, after all I've done for you?"

Not, "Why did you want to disgrace us?"

Just, "Why? Tell me about it. Why? Talk to me."

Which could be awfully difficult if you haven't been talking right along.

10

There's Always Sex, Isn't There?

Eventually we stopped having panels on drugs. Everyone had panels on drugs, and of all dreary worlds, the world of the addict is the most dreary.

But there is always sex. Always has been. Ever since Adam and Eve. And, if you believe Darwin, even before Adam and Eve, there had been sex. And isn't it fascinating? Each new crop of kids to come along discovers it all over again. It's like watching Columbus sight land every year.

If you sight land and then insist on wading ashore and exploring the new territory, you can get into trouble. This showed up regularly on the Triple-T segment. Girls wrote in wondering should they? Boys wrote in, amazingly enough, saying that their girls were so aggressive they didn't know what to do. One hot little plea came in the form of a telegram: "Dear TTTers. Please help me! I'm pregnant and I don't know what to do. Don't ask me to tell my parents. They'd kill me. Please help." It was signed "Terrified."

The Triple-T kids gave this one instant attention. They talked about it long and seriously and reached a decision. The girl should go immediately to the father of her child and tell him. If he wanted to marry her, and if she wanted to marry him, they should not drag their feet. They should get married.

I usually tried to keep my sticky fingers off the Triple-T segment, but I wasn't at all sure I liked this answer. Is being pregnant a good reason for taking out a marriage license? Aren't there other solutions? Do parents really kill a daughter who gets into trouble? Can't you go to an adult you trust and ask for guidance?

The Triple-T answer to the telegram was taped and I went to Sherm Payne with my worries and my doubts. Couldn't we retape the segment and get more flexibility into the answer? Couldn't we suggest some other things to this desperate girl?

"Let it go the way it is," Sherm decided. "Triple-T is supposed to be kids helping other kids. If this is what they believe, let them say it."

He was right. That's what we were supposed to be doing. We did it.

The day after the show went on the air the phone rang. It was a woman we'll call Mrs. X. She apologized for not calling sooner but said she'd been busy. "I'm the mother of the girl who sent that wire," she said.

There was no need to ask which wire.

"My daughter wanted me to take a nap while 'The Indispensables' was on yesterday." The woman managed a brief little laugh. "I don't take naps, and it made me uneasy. So I didn't stay in the room with her, but I listened, and after the Triple-T segment, I knew. She was crying. I think, maybe I'd guessed already."

We talked, and I could tell that Mrs. X was a terrific person. She'd done all the right things. She'd let the girl cry her cry and then tell her story, and she'd promised they'd work it out.

That girl was very lucky. She'd gone with the boy for two years, and her parents approved of him. She followed the Triple-T advice and told him, and they decided to be married. Of course they kept the baby. The parents didn't kill anybody; they helped. The couple went on to college, with a handsome son to keep their lives from getting stale.

Some of the grown-ups didn't like what they heard on that Triple-T segment, and we had letters about it. We also had letters on almost all of our panels on sex. What parents forget sometimes is that today almost everything is out in the open. Kids used to gather their funds of information—and misinformation—out behind the barn or in a corner of the girls' locker room. "Learning about it in the gutter" was the expression, although I never saw any serious discussions taking place in gutters. Gutters are very public and they tend to be damp. But there was a fantastic amount of nonsense being passed around when I was growing up. One friend, I recall, seriously believed that you could get pregnant if you kissed a boy "a lot." Not at all, said another, but if you sat on his lap . . .!

Kids today do not bother with this flapdoodle. They have the straight scoop. They know the language and they use it. It isn't always the language of love. Sometimes it's quite clinical. We had one panel on that birth control pill which was to make the sixties safe for sex. Our guest was a gynecologist of some distinction and, fortunately, tremendous poise.

"Suppose a boy called you," said one of the girls. "He's just gotten into town, see, and he wants a date tonight. And you like him real well. So you figure about ten you're going to be having intercourse with him. Would it do any good to take a pill at four?"

The doctor didn't flick an eyelash. He simply explained that it didn't work like that.

"I see," said the girl, and she went on to her next question.

She did not appear even slightly disappointed, and I knew she was only trying to get the facts and not to chart a course of conduct.

But she had asked an extremely outright question and she had used the word *intercourse* and television is a medium where bigger folk than she have been rapped on the knuckles for using expressions like *WC*.

I talked to the doctor afterward. I wanted to retape the bit and eliminate that word, and perhaps that question. He was against it. "That's the way they talk now," he told me. "Why change it? Besides, it's a good question. It's something kids ought to know. Maybe it'll keep some girl out of trouble."

We went on with the tape as it was, but we made one large mistake. We forgot to let the telephone operator in on the whole affair. The switchboard lighted up like twenty seven Christmas trees, and the operator frantically scribbled messages such as, "Mrs. Jones will never watch your filthy show again, and she won't let her children watch it, either."

"Did that girl really say that word?" asked the operator when she handed me the pile of messages.

"That's what she said."

"Wow!" said the operator.

"It was a hypothetical question," I told her.

"Wow, anyway!"

But why? At least the word has more than four letters. And, as the good doctor pointed out, it was an intelligent question. Maybe it did keep some girl out of trouble.

Sex education is another of the subjects that you can run through year after year. Most people are now pro, but there is much argument about how, and also how early. One of our young hostesses decided that however you approach the subject, you couldn't possibly give marks in it. It wouldn't do at all to flunk sex education!

One boy got us into a real tangle when he opted for sex education from the elementary school level on up. "Sex isn't any different from eating," he announced. "One day you suddenly find out you need it and you can't get along without it unless you want to flip your tree. But you'd better know how to control it, just like you control eating."

I spent hours taking calls on that one. What the boy was pleading for was early information, so you'd understand what was happening when that ton of bricks fell on you. All the parents heard was that the kids thought they had to have sex. The calls were miserable to handle. Again and again I'd hear myself suggesting that the parents talk, listen, communicate, keep in touch. And also, difficult as it might be, not lose their cool.

When Bishop Fulton Sheen came to Phoenix to take part in some special services at Luke Air Force Base, we planned an interview with him, but we sure didn't plan to ask him about sex. The man is a celibate and he's also a bishop and he's also a television personality. We figured we'd ask him about the changes in the church and also give him a chance to talk about his own television show.

For a while it looked as if we weren't going to get to ask him anything at all. Bishop Sheen was a house guest of Clare Boothe Luce while he was in town. He had converted her to Catholicism and he had baptized her, and the rumor was that she tended to be a mite possessive about him. I got several strong hints. Get out to Luke and try to meet him and talk with him.

The services at Luke were long and the chapel was filled. So was the area outside the chapel. I fought my way into the officers' club, which is where everything winds up anyway, and at last the press started to come in.

In spite of the flashbulbs popping, there was something Renaissance about the whole scene. There were people with

Bishop Sheen—members of the clergy—but you didn't think of it that way when you saw him in his purple cape and cap. He was being attended the way a prince might be attended.

I was way, way back, which is a position I get into a lot, so I climbed up onto a chair. I didn't want to miss any part of this. I had talked to several priests about the show. One of them spotted me and worked his way over. He had bad news. The bishop's schedule was tight, and besides Mrs. Luce hadn't seen him for some years. She wanted time to visit with him.

Win a few, lose a few. But I didn't get down from the chair. It was fascinating to watch the bishop; he started making his own path and the priests with him edged along behind. He saw me, teetering on my chair, and he came over. The crowd gave way in front of him. I climbed down and he asked, of all things, where I had gotten my hat. When I told him Great Falls, Montana, one of the clergymen explained, "This is the lady who produces the youth program you were going to be on."

The bishop looked pained. "I'm so sorry about that," he told me. "I've heard nice things about the program, but I haven't seen Clare for some time. But I am sorry." Then he smiled a wonderful smile. "What do you propose we do?" he asked.

One of the priests with him looked worried and made hurrying noises, but you don't hurry a bishop if he isn't in the mood.

"I propose we scoop you up and take you to the station to do the interview and then take you right back," I said quickly.

He thought this was a fine idea. We'd work out the details. He would let me know. I had visions of driving up to a side gate at the Luce house and picking up Bishop Sheen, who would be disguised as a gardner.

We didn't have to do anything cloak and dagger. The bishop managed things himself. He came in a long, black, properly clerical car with a chauffeur. Gay, a dark little sparkle of a girl, did the interview, together with Bill. They were in awe of this beautiful, alabaster man, and they edged into it carefully. As we had planned, they asked him about his television show and whether he missed doing it. They mentioned the changes in the church. Then, inevitably, they asked him what he thought about young people today.

He thought young people were fine. He wouldn't say a thing bad about them. Instead, he talked about the troubled times, not only in the church, but everywhere. The moral standards were changing in certain areas.

And there we were at sex, and there was Gay saying it was hard.

"It's always been hard," said His Excellency.

Gay shook her head. "It's harder today," she insisted. "It has to be harder than it was for our parents because everything is so much more accepted. And it's everywhere—the advertising, movies, magazines, you know?"

The bishop knew.

"But still," said Gay, "I think we're basically moral people, and even if it is accepted, if a girl gets pregnant before she's married, it can ruin her life. It's tough, and it's so much tougher on the girl than on the boy."

This is one of the great truths, no matter what the Women's Liberation ladies proclaim. The bishop didn't gainsay her.

"It isn't fair!" said Gay. There wasn't any audience in the studio. We were doing a special video tape. I don't think Gay would have opened up quite that way if there had been an audience. "A girl's no different than a boy," she said. "When a girl falls in love with a boy, no matter what she's been taught and no matter how high her standards are, when you're with that boy and you're out and the moon is shining and the boy tells you he loves you more than anything in the world, it's awfully hard to keep from . . . from . . ."

She didn't know what expression to use. She couldn't use that clinical term—not with Bishop Sheen.

The bishop touched one of her hands, and he put his other hand on Bill's. "There's one thing you have to remember," he said. "There's one thing I always tell young people who come to me with this problem. When a boy sees a girl who's very attractive to him, he falls in love with her physically. *Amour* moves into his brain right away. Immediately."

He turned to Bill. "When you see a girl, don't you look at her legs?" he asked.

Bill didn't like this. He turned red and didn't answer.

"Don't you?" demanded His Excellency.

Bill said, "I suppose."

Bishop Sheen turned back to Gay. "So a boy can love a girl right away and get over it just as fast and forget about it," he told her. "But when a girl falls in love with a boy, it takes a long time. She falls in love with the way he runs down the football field and the way he recites in class and the way he walks and the things he says. Last of all, she falls in love with him physically. When that happens, that's very dangerous, because when that happens she's ready to give herself to that boy. But it's not wrong. It's very human. God made her to love and to want love. That's why it's such a difficult thing, and it always has been. It was when I was a young man and when my grandfather was a young man. Always, it's difficult."

Gay looked at him with those big brown eyes and she said, so seriously, "But what do you do?"

He smiled. "You pray a lot, my dear," he said.

He left for Mrs. Luce's right after the interview and Gay, I firmly believe, went home to say her prayers. Next day she was back, laughing, and I think a little embarrassed about having been so open with His Excellency. I assured her that she was in good company. He has a reputation for inducing frankness in people.

The interview was a fair success when it was aired, although

Gay got embarrassed all over again. Then we didn't think much more about it until I realized that we had a medium-sized scandal going on the "Indispensables" set.

To be precise, it was not on the set. It was one of the kids who hung around, and who hung around in a very noticeable way. He was tall and very handsome, and we seldom finished a show without having him nab the prettiest guest and sweep her off to admire the wonders of Phoenix.

After two telephone calls in rapid succession from two irate parents, I discovered that the tour for visiting fireladies did not include the Superstition Mountains or the cacti in Papago Park, but it was a ritual. This suave seventeen-year-old would suggest a movie, and then a late supper. Late suppers are terribly sophisticated and romantic and the girls almost always accepted.

So first there would be the movie.

Immediately after the movie, there would be the discovery that the junior grade Lothario had left most of his money at home. A stop at the house would be in order. Not only did he need to get money, but he wanted the girl to meet his mom and dad.

Being invited to meet Mom and Dad is even more romantic than a late supper. They trotted along, wide-eyed and eager to make a good impression.

Dad was almost always out of town on business.

Mom was almost always asleep. She liked to play golf at dawn, so she went to bed early.

Lothario, j.g., would open the front door and call gently, "Mom? Dad?"

Naturally, no one would answer.

"Darn!" he'd say. "They must have gone out." Or, "Darn! They're asleep."

The next step in the ritual was the short walk down a path to Lothario's room so he could pick up his money. The house had wings running off here and there, and Lothario had one wing all to himself. There was a terrace outside his bedroom. Inside there was a bed, a bureau, and exactly one chair. So when he opened the door and went in, he promptly sat in that chair.

The girl could either hover on the terrace like an uncertain hen, or come in and sit on the bed. Numbers of them, fearful of seeming rude, came in and sat on the bed.

There were a few casual remarks, very smooth, and then the little ladies got hugged. What happened after the hug depended on how rude the little ladies felt like being then. The two little ladies whose parents called me had been very rude indeed, and the parents seemed to feel that I was responsible for the boy's actions. He had, after all, met the girls because of the TV show.

I was considering ways and means of having the boy barred from the studio, and also wondering whether or not I had better call that golf-playing mother, when one of our hostesses came giggling to me with a variation on the tale of young Lothario. He had, it seemed, attached himself to a real mite of a lass who came not quite to his shoulder. She went through the movie bit and fell for the line about going home to meet Mother, and she came in off the terrace and sat down on the bed. Then, when she found herself with her nose mashed against the boy's shirt front, she said, "If you don't let go of me, I'm going to bite you right on the navel."

It worked like a charm. She was home well before midnight.

Perhaps she had prayed, as the good bishop had suggested; the remark was inspired. On the other hand, she may have had little need for divine intervention just then. Lothario, j.g., had forgotten one of the bishop's pearls of wisdom; it takes time for a girl to fall in love.

11

Terror

Occasionally people talk about their fears. When they do, they are like jewelers arranging rings on a piece of velvet. They bring out the most interesting ones. They display them carefully, turning them this way and that so that they can be admired. Young Rich admits to being afraid of the dark in his mother's backyard. No other dark holds terrors for him. The dreaded things lurk only in that shadowy strip between his mother's kitchen door and the place where her trash can resides. Mary cannot get within ten feet of a horse or a mule. Addie will walk countless flights of stairs to avoid a self-service elevator. Wilson can swim only in a pool. For him, the ocean seethes with sharks. Wilson has never met a shark, but he knows that they are there and they bristle with teeth.

The ordinary phobias aren't much mentioned. It is dull to be afraid of snakes, mice, closed places or open places, and it is unpatriotic to be afraid of dogs. Only postmen are permitted to be afraid of dogs.

The universal terror is scarcely ever discussed. When the ultimate disgrace is to lose your cool, very few people will admit to stage fright. But fear of the audience—or the camera or the mike or whatever represents the audience—is always there. Anyone in television has seen and experienced yards and yards and acres and miles of stage fright. Amateurs surely get it. Some professionals get it sometimes and some professionals get it all the time. It was the scourge of "The Indispensables." The first two months of any season were alive with butterflies. Lips twitched and knees trembled and kids bumped into things and fell over things. One girl sneezed whenever she got upset; her first appearance on camera looked like a commercial for a hay fever remedy. She wound up her performance by saying, "Sorry, I always sneeze when I'm nervous," and then covering her face and bursting into tears.

The only thing that kept the crew sane during these trying periods was the knowledge that it would get better. The only thing that kept the cast from deserting in a body was the realization that cameras do not pick up the tics and the shivers. Once the kids knew that they didn't look as scared as, in fact, they were, and that they would get through a taping session without being struck by lightning or booed by the audience, the days became easier and the nights more restful.

But then there was Bob, and for a long, long time things did not get easier for him.

He came on the show for the first time like a gentle young Solomon. He was one of four student body presidents who sat on a panel with an outstanding, and most controversial, judge. Two young punks in town had ganged up on a third boy and beaten him. They had used their fists until he was down, and then they had used their feet. One of the kicks landed in the wrong place and the boy died. One of the boys had a long history of nasty incidents involving fists and feet and other means of persuasion. Once he had sent a ten-year-old girl to the hospital. He was not beloved by his schoolmates or by anyone else I ever knew.

After their victim died, the two boys were tried and convicted in the judge's court. The town was aghast when the judge suspended their sentences and let them go free. The knowledge of what they had done, he said, would be their punishment—a punishment that would last all of their lives.

Kids generally stick up for other kids, but no one stuck up for these two. The three other student body presidents on that panel fried the judge. He sat defending his decision in sentences that he never got to finish. They cut in on him. They cut him down. But cool, calm, mature Bob did not. Not that Bob had one good word to say for boys who stomp other boys to death. He did protest, however, that the judge's ruling might be a wise one. Surely it had been one made with hope and great good faith.

Bob never shouted, but he stood his ground. He kept his calm and his compassion. It takes a special brand of courage to go against your peers that way. I was impressed with Bob.

No long after that panel, I lost the boy who did our Triple-T segment. I remembered Bob. Anyone who could be that calm and that wise would be terrific for the Triple-T. And he was a student body president, so he had to have a following. He'd mentioned something about being on the baseball team. We could use a back-up host for the sports interviews. I called his high school.

The principal of the school couldn't say enough good about Bob. He was bright, and although he was shy, he liked the other kids and the other kids liked him. The principal gave me a telephone number to call.

My first attempt to contact Bob by telephone was a flat failure. The phone at Bob's house was answered by someone with a juicy baritone that could not have belonged to a high school senior. It takes years to develop that kind of voice and that much charm. But when I asked for Bob the charm went away.

The man said something like, "Oh? Bob? Yeah! Well, he's not home. I'll tell him you called."

A day passed and nothing happened. I called again. This time I got a woman who said she was Bob's mother. She didn't try to snow me with charm, but she was very sweet. I waited while she found a pencil and paper and wrote down the number of the station.

Bob called the day after that. We made an appointment and he came into the station. By that time I had moved my office up from APS and had a cozy little room across the hall from the big studio, right between the water cooler and the place where the coffee urn perked. The traffic got a little heavy at times, but I never had a chance to get lonely. Bob found me there. His hands were trembling when he came in. This surprised me. He waited patiently through four interruptions and one telephone call and he calmed down. We talked about him. He was good to listen to. He knew a little bit about a lot of things and a lot about baseball. He told me that he had lost his father when he was a baby. The man I talked to on the telephone must have been his stepfather. His eyes wandered away when he said that, and he hurried on to talk about his ambition, which was to be an engineer.

Sitting in that little office, I recalled a boy who had been in my Sunday school class the second year in Great Falls. His father had been to any number of exclusive, expensive military schools and had learned any number of useful things, but he did not know how to behave like a human being. The boy had come Sunday after Sunday, stoically ignoring the bruises and bumps his father had inflicted on him. He had always looked away when fathers were discussed. He had looked away as Bob did when his stepfather was mentioned.

So Bob had problems with his stepfather. I was sorry about that, but it was no reason not to take him on "The Indispensables." He was everything we needed. He'd be fine on the Triple-T segment and he had the background for sports.

He turned out to be both terrific and terrified. He went on the first week in the usual cloud of butterflies. He was stiff with fright the week after that and the week after that and the week after that. I couldn't understand it. It hadn't shown the day of the panel with the judge. Besides, he was a student body president, which meant that he had to stand up on his two feet at fairly regular intervals and talk to groups of kids.

"Why did you run for student body president?" I asked him one day.

"I had to," he said. "The other boy who was running for the office was wrong for it."

That was as much as he would say about it. Indeed, he said very little about anything that was truly close to him. He had a home and a mother, but we never saw them. He was nice to everyone and everyone liked him, but he had a wall around himself ten feet high and three feet thick, and he wouldn't open the gate. He sat inside all alone, and when it was time to tape a show or to meet new people, he trembled.

Allie Chalmers did the Triple-T segment with him and she adored him. She tried to climb over that wall. She invited him to her home, but he wouldn't go. Bob lived on the edge of the wrong side of town. Allie, whose daddy owned a chain of restaurants, lived very much on the right side of town. "I don't belong there," Bob would say, and that would be that.

Allie didn't give up. She politely ignored his sweating and shaking before we began to tape, and once she and Bob were on and going over their Triple-T problems, they were both great. Bob seemed to have a very special understanding of kids who were in trouble.

The boys Bob interviewed on the sports segment loved him. They didn't notice that he was scared, because most of them were also scared. They only knew that he was good, he knew his stuff and he made them look good.

After a while we began to use Bob on panels. This was easier. There were other kids in there with him. He wasn't quite so uptight, but he was still nervous.

Then, one quiet winter afternoon, he came into the studio to do a special video tape recording. I have forgotten who the guest was. I only remember that that afternoon, for the first time, Bob was not trembling or stiff or breathing deeply to put down the butterflies. He went over his notes for the interview calmly. The guest hadn't arrived. There was no audience except me and a couple of preoccupied technicians.

I thought we'd had a breakthrough. I thought that Bob had at last licked that terrible stage fright.

"We're going to have Joe Garagiola next Monday," I told Bob. "Want to do the interview?"

He looked up from his notes. "I can't. I have to be in court on Monday."

I didn't think too much about this. Like many cities, Phoenix has a student court, and Bob was much involved in it. Joe Garagiola is one of the most obliging of human beings. I whipped across to my office and made a quick telephone call. Yes, Joe could make it on Tuesday.

Back to Bob. "We can get Garagiola on Tuesday," I said. "How about it? You'd be good with him."

He shook his head. "I have to be in court on Tuesday, too."

I didn't want to make a second telephone call. Garagiola would think I'd flipped. I sat down and watched Bob pace back and forth looking at his pad, then looking up, then looking back at his pad. Suddenly he said, "Jane, you'd think you'd be afraid, but you aren't."

I didn't answer him. I hoped that perhaps a gate was opening in that ten-foot wall around Bob.

"You really aren't afraid," he said. "He locked me in a cage when I was six years old and he'd never let me out. If I tried to get away, he hurt my mom."

The telephone rang in my office across the hall. I let it ring. "Cage?" I said.

"The backyard," Bob explained. "There's a fence around it. He put me in the backyard and I couldn't get out."

"Your stepfather?"

Bob nodded.

"Did he . . . hurt you, too, Bob?"

"Sure he did. Lots of times. But this time I took it away from him."

"What did you take away?"

"The gun. He had a gun. I came home from school and my mom was on the floor. He'd beaten her up again and he said this time he was going to kill her."

Bob took a deep breath, not looking at me or at anything in particular in that big studio. Then he went on: "I said to him, 'You're not going to hurt her anymore and you can't scare me anymore.' I went at him and he told me to stop or he'd shoot, but I wasn't afraid. I told him he wasn't going to hurt her anymore, and he gave me the gun. He handed it to me."

Bob turned his back. I couldn't tell whether he was crying or only breathing very hard. I got up and went across the hall to the coffee urn. Kids shouldn't drink coffee, but there are exceptions to every rule.

Bob didn't like the coffee. He made a face when he tasted it and he held it in his mouth for a minute before he swallowed. Probably it was too hot. Just as well. Physical sensations can bring you back to earth, even if they're not pleasant.

Bob sipped a little more. "So I can't do the interview with Joe Garagiola next Monday or Tuesday," he said. "I'll be in court testifying against my stepfather."

Our guest arrived. I don't know how he managed, but Bob

did the interview and did it well. Afterward, I told him so and asked him if he'd like a coke. I figured if he wanted to talk more, he'd accept the invitation. He did. He told me the whole long, sad, messy story. He told about the long years with the stepfather who hated him and punished him and hurt his mother. But now the years were over.

Bob went to court the next week. I don't know what the charge against the stepfather was—assault, I imagine, or assault with intent to kill. He got off with a suspended sentence. I was afraid at first that Bob's mother might follow a pattern that is classic with women who marry brutes. I was afraid she might take the stepfather back. She didn't. She filed for divorce and the case went through without a hitch. She got custody of Bob's little half-sister, whom Bob loved dearly, and Bob got a part-time job and hung around his house a lot because the stepfather moved into an apartment across the street.

"Get the locks changed," I advised him.

"I did that the first day," he said.

Bob held himself together for a week or two after the court appearance, then came unglued. He fluffed and fumbled and some days he didn't seem to know who his guests were. Once I found him in my office pounding on the wall with his fist. "I can't do anything right," he groaned. "I can't do one darned thing right."

This was too much for little Allie Chalmers. She moved in on him like Clara Barton. She made him go places with her. She told her family about him and she dragged him home with her and her family loved him.

Then Phyllis Diller came to town, and we were set to do an interview with her at the Star Theater. Allie was all excited about it. Bob stiffened up like an overstarched shirt. "At Buster Bonoff's Star Theater?" he said. "Phyllis Diller? Me? Say, I don't think . . ."

"Rats!" said Allie. "It'll be fun. Besides, it'll be on film.

Don't worry. It can be edited."

So Bob trailed Allie and me and the cameraman and the sound technician to that special room in the theater where the stars meet the press.

Phyllis Diller has made her fortune by pretending to be a gargoyle. She is not a gargoyle. She is a lady—a pretty one. The day we met her, her hair was not standing on end in the famous dishmop style. She was beautifully coiffured. Her dress was soft and becoming; her boots were neat and came only to her ankles. She grinned an ear-to-ear grin at the kids, plopped down in the middle of the sofa, and pulled Allie down on one side of her and Bob on the other.

Allie couldn't take her eyes off that hair. She had expected something so different, and she said so.

"The fright-wig bit started because I tipped my hair," said Miss Diller. "I tipped it before anyone else started tipping. I did a good job. I wrecked it was what I did. The doctor told me to brush it straight up to try to bring it back. I brushed and brushed and then I looked in the mirror. Early monster. I kept it."

On the subject of boots and weird clothes, Miss Diller was slightly amused. She had started the whole thing. At least, she had been going around looking like a cast-off Raggedy Ann doll long before anyone else. "Now I'm voguish!" she complained. "It's disgusting!"

Bob sat uneasily through this girl-chat. Miss Diller hit a period and stopped to put a cigarette into a long holder. Even the American Cancer Society would approve of the way Phyllis Diller uses a cigarette. For her, it is a prop, or perhaps a weapon. It's great to wave around in the air or to jab at things. I never saw her light it.

Bob watched her firm hands manipulating cigarette and holder. "Miss Diller," he said, "it's so wonderful that you never get nervous when you have to appear before big groups of people. You don't get nervous, do you?"

She looked at him. It may be that she looked deeper than most people look and that she saw more. "No," she said. "I really don't get nervous. I don't get nervous at all. I think you could call it *panic!*"

The raucous Diller laugh boomed out and the cigarette holder swept the air and Bob almost fell off the sofa.

"Listen," said Miss Diller, "anybody gets nervous. When you have to go into a room full of people you don't know well, you get nervous. If you didn't, you'd have to be either stupid or dead. Of course you get nervous. You know that everybody in that room knows everybody else, but you don't know anyone. You know that everybody is dressed better than you are and they have all the smart lines. Sure, you're scared. Unless you're a complete idiot, you get nervous."

Bob stared as this sophisticated woman went on talking. She told about how it was when she was a youngster. She talked about first dates, and the agony of trying to keep your cool and knowing that you were blowing it. She talked about her own children and how much she cared for them and how close they were. She wanted to understand them. They were a new generation, and she wanted so to understand them.

"Don't you think young people today have more problems than before?" said Bob.

"All young people have had problems," she said. "They're insurmountable problems. And all young people are sensitive. You have to take it one day at a time. Don't you think I've had problems?" She laughed again. "We all have problems, but we can't dwell on them. One thing the kids mustn't lose, and that's a sense of humor. Without that, you're in trouble!"

After the interview, we drove back to the station together.

"How does she know?" said Allie. "Most grown-ups don't remember."

"How does she know what?" said Bob.

"All that stuff about everybody else having better clothes and knowing everybody else and knowing what to say," Allie explained.

"But you never feel that way," Bob protested. "You've got everything." He didn't say it as if he resented it. It was only a statement of things as he saw them.

Allie set him straight. What she had, according to Allie, was five pounds too much weight and a real talent for saying kooky things at the wrong time. And she was scared of people, too, lots of times.

Bob was stunned, but happy. He might be out there in left field, but he wasn't alone. Allie was with him, and maybe all the other kids in Phoenix.

It would be tidy to report that after vanquishing his stepfather, and after his talk with Phyllis Diller, Bob turned into the most poised Indispensable of them all. But life is not tidy. Bob continued to be stiff and shy with strangers. However, to an extent the interview with Miss Diller was a turning point for him. He did try to take things one day at a time. He opened up the gate in that big high wall that surrounded him and he let in a few people. The last hour before taping continued to be torture for him, but he learned to handle it well. He learned not to show it. He hung in there and finished the season, and later he came back and did guest appearances. Bill Heywood, a disc jockey who came on the show as permanent host in 1969, loved working with him. He is so nice. He is also one of the bravest kids I've ever met.

It's easy to forget, but if you don't know what terror is, you don't know one thing about courage.

12

Ooops!

The trouble with the English language is that it will never stand still. And kids are no help. They take perfectly respectable, stolid words which have been in Webster for generations and they shove them around. They spangle them with special meanings, and what often results is a *double-entendre*—the *entendre* of which is single to anyone under twenty-one.

With three kids in residence at our house, I surely knew this. We had some adult guests who did not. There was the wonderful little Save-the-Elm lady in Great Falls, for example, who got tangled up with the word *horny*.

Now *horny* is a very proper word. Little boys catch horny toads. Working men get horny, or calloused, hands. So what's wrong with *horny*? Plenty.

I don't know where the Save-the-Elm lady encountered the word. She did not have children. She was emotionally involved with trees and came on "The Indispensables" to protest the straightening of Seventeenth Street because if the city straightened Seventeenth Street they would have to remove an ancient and honorable elm. She had reached that age of security when you doubt not that your cause is just; the age sets in somewhere between fifty-five and ninety. She was pink of cheek and quivering with indignation at the thought that anyone could be heartless enough to uproot that elm, or even to lop off a single branch. Hatted and gloved and with her lorgnette on a silver chain around her neck, she exuded respectability and outrage. She knew the history of the tree and she let us have it, knothole by knothole. Then she told us of her well-bred fury when she read the newspaper account of plans to remove the tree and straighten the street. "My dear," she said to me, "I was so upset I was absolutely horny!"

There had been some stirrings in the audience. They stopped. The kids froze for about two seconds and I heard one of the cameramen gasp. Then George, bless him, blurbled something about an oak that grew in front of his house. The tree lady was most partial to oaks, and liked maples as well, and we finished the interview in a burst of praise for all trees everywhere. Joyce Kilmer would have been enchanted.

Because George was so quick, and because the tree lady was such a monument of elegance and good taste, most of the souls who were watching the show that day must have decided they hadn't heard what they thought they'd heard. We had no telephone calls. But we did have a postmortem.

"You have to tell her," George said to me. "She can't go around saying things like that."

"But she didn't mean that!" I cried.

"I know it and you know it," said George, "but she doesn't know it. Somebody's got to tell her."

I couldn't. None of us could. How can you explain to a lady who wears dove-colored gloves and a lorgnette what the current teen interpretation of *horny* is? No way.

Stud is another of those goodies. I got into trouble with *stud*. In Montana, it was usual to call a boy a stud. It didn't mean much, except that he was a nice boy, handsome and masculine, and the girls liked him. For years I went happily along calling handsome, masculine men studs. Then I used the word in the presence of a friend from California. I was talking about Barry Goldwater, in fact, and he is handsome and masculine enough to decorate any landscape.

"Great scott, Jane!" exploded my California friend. "You can't mean that the man's a stud. I'm sure he's very respectable. Besides, he's a Republican!"

I couldn't figure what this outburst was all about until my friend outlined the plot of *Midnight Cowboy* for me. Now I do try not to call people studs, or to say that anyone is hustling anyone else. In my ignorance, I thought hustling was giving someone a rush—asking for a lot of dates.

In a way it is, but only in a way.

Number is another weirdie. A number is one or two or ten. A number is also a very attractive girl. A number is what is printed on your telephone dial. And it can also be a marijuana cigarette.

Not that all of the *in* expressions have double or triple or quadruple meanings. Some are only bewildering to the uninitiated adult. I barked my shins on *right on* not long ago. "They're right on," said Cathy, talking about a new rock group.

"Right on what?" said I, fearfully.

She gave me that look kids give adults. "They're with it," she explained. "They're groovey."

Okay, okay. But *right on* followed by nothing gives you the feeling that you've missed a step in the dark and fallen on your face.

After skittering around countless bloopers on the air, you learn not to use words unless you're sure you know and approve of all sixteen possible variations of meaning, including the variation some hep kid thought up last week. You also pray that your guests will exercise similar caution. But there are so many other ways to have accidents.

In Montana, things were relatively simple. The studio was small. The sets were stark basic. Outside of "Romper Room" chairs and falling drapes, there were few accidents. In Phoenix we had more scope. We had a bigger studio. We had more accidents.

Cast numbers were especially good for accidents. Emmett, our artist, liked cast numbers because they gave him the opportunity to whip up clever little sets. For "Don't Fence Me In" he put up—what else?—a small fence. It was a pretty thing, white pickets surrounding a lawn of fake grass with some plastic daisies. In the middle of the number one of the girls fell through the fence. She scraped her shin and bruised her dignity, but she was a trouper. She missed only six words of the lyrics. One of the boys picked her up. She was not bleeding badly and the group finished gallantly and nearly on time. You couldn't hear them. The audience had broken up. We were taping the show, and we could have done the cast number over, but we didn't. If watching someone fall through a fence is that amusing, we would use it.

The gazebo incident could not be used. The gazebo was Emmett's dream. He had always wanted to build one, but had never had a good excuse. "The Indispensables" gave him his excuse, and he produced a charming, mid-Victorian structure. We arranged the kids artfully on this lovely creation and they began to sing. In the middle of that number, one of the girls fell off the gazebo and not only scraped her shins and bruised her dignity, but showed her panties. A girl can be altogether comfortable in the briefest of bikinis, but she goes to pieces if anyone sees her panties. We redid the gazebo number. Any other course would have been cruel and unthinkable.

We had little trouble with guests. We usually sat them down, so they couldn't fall, and very few people willfully go on the air and blow an interview. There were only two in the history of

"The Indispensables" who did this. One was an exchange student in Great Falls and the other was Michael Parks, who was the object of much interest when he came to Phoenix because of his television series, "Bronson."

There was some excuse for the exchange student. He was not just any old student. He was a visiting prince. His father was a chieftain in Nigeria and he had been sent to the United States to catch up on our advanced technology. What he encountered was our advanced prejudice, and he came into the studio in a state of cold rage. He looked like a handsome, ebony statue.

I did the interview with the boy. I had read up on Nigeria and I wanted him to talk about his country. He was not talking. He was furious at the white man—and also at the white woman with all her nosey questions.

I shifted to neutral. The weather is always a safe subject. "Do you find it cold here?" I asked him. "Were you able to bring enough warm clothes with you?"

The weather is not always a safe subject. He may have thought I was offering a secondhand overcoat. He reared back and snapped, "I would freeze to death before I took anything from a white man." Then he stalked out of the studio, leaving me to flub my way through a discussion of Nigeria with nary a Nigerian in sight.

But I forgave him. He was young, and upset.

Michael Parks was not upset. Off camera he was charming. He was agreeable. He was Bronson, the gentle wanderer. Yes, he said, people did think he looked like James Dean. They were always saying so. And no, he wouldn't mind being asked about this on the air.

So when we were ready and we went on the air, I said, "People say that you look like James Dean. Do you think so?"

"James Dean is alive," announced Parks.

"Well, but . . ."

"James Dean is alive. He's pumping gas at a little station up in northern California."

"Mr. Parks, do you . . . ?"

"He's alive and well and pumping gas."

We never got off it. Six whole minutes of anyone insisting that James Dean is alive and well and pumping gas is as interesting as a recitation from the telephone book. Less interesting. You usually find what you're looking for in the telephone book.

You live through these things and the sun does go down and you do sleep, finally, and the sun comes up and you begin again. With Dr. Ronald Dante, I was not sure this nice arrangement would continue for all involved.

Dante is not as famous as Winston Churchill or Richard M. Nixon, but he is famous. He hypnotizes people. He does it in nightclubs and he does it well. He can convince a girl who resembles a mugwump gone wrong that she is really Elizabeth Taylor, and she will then fare forth into the audience to dazzle the men and to flash her million-carat personality. His appearances in Phoenix were the sensation of the Valley of the Sun. Kids who were old enough to go to nightclubs paid stiff cover charges to be hypnotized or to watch. Kids who weren't old enough to go to nightclubs wished they were, and the kids on "The Indispensables" urged and pleaded and had their friends write letters because they wanted Dante on the show.

Hypnotism is a strange thing. Some people swear by it. They say it's the only way to diet. Other people are scared to death of it, and I'm in there with the cowards. Drill my teeth or take out my appendix if you must, but leave my mind alone.

But there was much pressure and pleading. I temporized. I wavered. I talked to the sponsor. It was okay with him. I went to the station manager. It was okay with him. At last, I went to Dante.

He was living north of Phoenix in a big, comfortable, Arizona rambling house. It could have been the home of a bank president or the head of the pickle factory, except that bank presidents do not put black skulls on their front doors. The doorbell did not ring; it rasped in an unearthly fashion.

A houseboy in a white jacket opened the door. When I said my name he stepped back so that I could come in. The door whooshed closed behind me and I blinked at a dim foyer and at cool, dim rooms stretching away on the left and right. Air conditioning hummed in a quiet, costly way. I followed the houseboy to the right, down two steps into a living room, and there was Dante.

This Dante did not look a smidge like that gloomy gentleman who once lived in Florence and wrote long, difficult poems. This Dante looked like the playboy of the western world. He wore a handsome sports shirt artfully opened to expose a handsome chest. He was well barbered, well manicured, well tanned, and surrounded by advisors and by scrapbooks. According to the scrapbooks he knew everyone in the world who was worth knowing. I think he had not met Queen Elizabeth, but almost everyone else was represented, and the names were duly dropped.

"I'll come on your show," he told me.

"Not so fast," I wanted to say, but that would have been rude. Instead I said, "There are a few things we have to get straight first."

"Such as?"

"You will not hypnotize any of my kids."

One eyebrow went up. He looked me over as if I had suddenly broken out pregnant. "How many kids do you have?"

"I mean the Indispensables," I told him. "They're teenagers, and I'm responsible for them. Hypnosis scares me. Can you bring your own subject?"

"I never have trouble getting volunteers," he said.

"And you cannot hypnotize anyone on the air. It's against FCC regulations. You'll have to do it *before* we start."

This was true. The FCC is leery of hypnotists. They may have visions of Dante or one of his colleagues doing his bit on a national network and turning us all into zombies.

Dante told me he knew the rules as well as I did. Then he offered to hypnotize me. I was, he said, rather tense.

I grew more tense. In truth, I was a little frightened. I wanted to get through and get out. I did. I did it so quickly that we had about seventeen telephone calls afterward to tidy up the details, but we were set. "The Indispensables" would have the great Dante.

Bob, our program director, blanched when he learned that one of Dante's props would be a hunk of concrete weighing four hundred pounds and liberally laced with rocks. I assured him that Dante would see to having it delivered to the studio.

"But what about the floor?" asked Bob.

We had a brand new finish on the studio floor. It was terribly expensive white stuff which had been applied like paint and had dried so that it looked like marble. Bob had been trying to get it for two years. Having succeeded, he was as protective of it as a hen with one chick.

"Oh, I hardly think they'll drop the thing on the floor," I told him. "They'll put it down gently. They use it all the time in nightclubs."

Bob didn't look happy, but he agreed that I was making sense.

The great day arrived.

Dante arrived.

The chunk of cement arrived.

We had a lot of high-school kids in the audience, and mobs of college kids. The Indispensables were up front twittering like birds. Dante and his entourage impressed the fool out of everyone.

Before we started taping, we had to have a warm-up, and Dante had to get his volunteer and put her under. He called me outside to discuss this, and then didn't discuss it. He only put his hand on my shoulder and told me everything would be all right. Then he went back into the studio.

I followed him in, and Cathy stared at me the way you stare at someone who's forgotten to button her blouse. "Jane!" she said.

Paul laughed.

I looked down. My buttons were buttoned. My skirt was not turned up. My shoes matched. What was wrong?

"Oh, Jane!" said Cathy. She reached out and took something from my shoulder, where Dante had touched me. The something was a button—the kind of button that advises you to vote for Wintergreen for president. Only this button said, "I just slept with Doctor Dante."

That is a special kind of graffiti.

I did not have time to shoot Dr. Dante through the head right then, or to kick him in the shins, because he was up in front of the audience doing his thing with a pretty little girl from ASU. He rubbed the back of her neck and talked to her softly, and she was gone—real gone.

Then it was time.

Emmett had done a marvelous portrait of Dante, and this came on first. Then we had a smoke effect drift up over the portrait and we went to a dissolve and then the camera was in close on Dante's face. It was very effective.

The camera pulled back to show the ASU girl, and Dante snapped his fingers. The girl went stiff. Dante lifted her and put her head on one chair and her feet on the other. The rest of her stayed rigid as a pine plank. She sagged not a bit.

This is a standard trick. What came next was not so standard.

Dante signaled to our two athletic guests, who had offered to handle his dreadful hunk of concrete. The boys grunted and huffed and hefted the concrete off the floor and put it down gently, gently on the girl's stomach.

Dante picked up a sledge hammer.

I was in the control room, and I couldn't bear to look. I turned around. But I heard the hideous crash that came through on the audio when the sledge hammer hit the concrete.

Bob cursed.

I still couldn't look. "Is that girl all right?" I asked.

"She's fine," said Bob, "but he ruined my beautiful floor!"

We had a show every year where we reviewed our most amusing bloopers. We didn't use Dante on it. He hadn't goofed. He had done exactly what he'd set out to do. Besides, it would have been so painful to Bob to see the floor go again.

13

Some Interviews You Get

A spontaneous demonstration can be a fair amount of work. When Bobby Kennedy was scheduled to spend a day in Phoenix in the spring of 1968, mighty were the preparations. The Indispensables were in on them. Kennedy was big with many of the kids and especially with Cathy, who fairly fainted with joy at the thought that she might get to do an interview with the senator. We were on the receiving end of many telephone calls from Washington, and this was exciting all by itself. We did our best; it's a nice thing to do, even if it does involve racing about and making endless local phone calls. We got one of the best musical groups in the valley to appear at the airport. We also rounded up a slew of kids. There might have been a slew of kids anyway, but we did make sure they had the word. I don't think the musicians were all that political, but the networks were covering the arrival and any young musician thirsts after TV exposure.

In return for all of this we asked for—we did not demand, we only requested—an interview with Bobby Kennedy for "The Indispensables."

The Kennedy plane was due at Sky Harbor in Phoenix at two

that afternoon. It touched down at four. The whole day was bollixed up.

"We won't get the interview," I said to one of the Kennedy aides after the plane landed.

He looked at that crowd of kids who had been waiting in the desert sun. He saw the musical group playing their little hearts out. "You'll get it," he said. "This is great."

I wanted to believe him, but I had my doubts. The airport that afternoon was out. We weren't ready and even if we had been, we couldn't have done it. The senator was running too late. There was a tour of the city scheduled, and after that a dinner which would take place beside the pool at the Arizona Biltmore.

The aide and I decided that we'd try for that evening, just before dinner.

The camera crew set up in a room at the Biltmore that we'd used for other interviews. After Cathy and Paul talked with the senator, the men could move out to cover Kennedy's speech at the dinner. Bill Sherman, head cameraman, and the others got in early, which was a good thing because the grounds of the Biltmore quickly became jammed with people. There were thousands there. Some of them had paid $50 or $100 or whatever it was to come in, watch the St. John's Indians perform, eat the dinner, and listen to the senator. The rest had just come. They were young and old and fat and thin and tall and short and they were mashed together so tightly that if one person stood on his tiptoes, everyone around him also went up—including me, because I wasn't in the $100 section. I was squirming through the crowd trying to find Cathy, who was determined to watch the senator's arrival. She did watch it, too.

Kennedy came, surrounded by security men, but the crowd surged at him, reaching, grasping, trying to touch him. A woman next to me squealed the way bobby-soxers used to squeal at Frank Sinatra.

"Look! Look!" She had something in her hand and she brushed it against my face. I felt goose bumps come up on my arms.

"Is that his hair?" I asked.

She was so excited. She was so pleased. "Yes. It's from his head! It's from his head!"

"You trying to scalp him?"

She looked at me as if I were a slug in her salad. "You don't belong here," she told me. "Why don't you get out of here?"

I was trying. I edged and pushed and bumped up against Cathy, who was in a great state of nerves, anxiety, and anticipation.

"I'm going around to the room to make sure the cameras are set up," she said.

"They're set up," I told her.

She went anyway.

At least I knew where she was—if only she would stay put. The crowd eased and opened up a bit, and I got into the clear. The senator was in the clear, too, and talking to the Indians, who had their own little section in front of the hotel where they could wait before going on to perform.

I started around the big building toward the back—toward the pool and the tables. It was dark, with only little amber lights gleaming at ankle level along the path. I heard footsteps behind me, and a voice said, "You look like you're running away from something."

I stopped and looked back. "I just want to get away from that crowd," I told the man who stood near me on the path.

"Yes?"

"These people are killing each other to try to touch just a human being," I said.

I could not really see his face, but I am sure he smiled. "That's true," he said, "but they're people all the same." He put out his hand and said, "I'm Bobby Kennedy."

I took the hand and murmured some inane thing, and then he was suddenly removed. There were two men beside him and they physically took him away. One moved in against me and pushed, very gently. At the same time, he took the senator's arm. The other man was on Kennedy's other side, and they walked him off, flanking him. They were worried about more than his hair.

I got into the area near the press table and Bill Sherman zipped out and grabbed me. "Are we going to get him now?" he asked. "We've got to know. It's going to take time to move the equipment out to catch the speech."

I was not quite sure. The head of the Democratic Party for the state had said so. The aide I'd talked to at the airport had seemed hopeful. But there was one man who seemed to be ram-rodding the entire project, and he had said maybe. Maybe is not by any means an ironclad promise. I saw him coming and I got in his path.

He was very, very big. He was worried. He was going some-where and did not want to stop. Someone said, "This is the producer on 'The Indispensables.' She has to know."

"Do we get the interview with Senator Kennedy?" I asked him.

Maybe I shouldn't have asked. Not then. The man was exhausted. The day had been a killer. And he had doubtless had a gullet full of people who wanted to know things.

He didn't answer. Instead, he grabbed my shoulders and shook me. My head bobbled back and forth. I hadn't been shaken like that since I was a naughty five-year-old. "What did I tell you this afternoon?" he demanded.

He shook me some more.

Cathy materialized out of the night. Paul came running from someplace. But neither of the kids knew what to do about it. No one knew what to do about it. I thought it might be a good idea to cry, but I hate crying in public.

"What did I tell you?" he asked again.

He stopped shaking me.

My brains settled and I remembered what he had actually said that afternoon. He had said, "We're not assuring it, but it looks very good."

I was switched if I'd repeat it. "Are you an attorney?" I asked.

He had, in fact, gotten his degree five years before.

"I thought so," I told him. "I feel like I'm being interrogated on the stand."

This infuriated him still further. "You lose him!" he snapped. "You absolutely lose him!"

Somebody flew to the head table, where the Kennedys were sitting with about eighteen people. I crept to the press table to hide, and the reporters there told me that it was tough. They knew it was tough, but you had to take things like that sometimes. Cathy was beside me pleading, "Jane, he's a terrible, terrible man, but please be nice to him. We have to get the senator."

An emissary from the head table arrived with a promise— an absolute promise. We would get the senator, but not that night. We would get him at the airport the next morning.

It was as well that Cathy and Paul didn't do the interview that night. They were upset, and so were large numbers of the people who had crowded onto the Biltmore grounds. Roped off in one corner, well away from the $100-a-plate areas, there were mobs of kids. Many of them must have been pro-Kennedy, but a goodly number were anti-Kennedy, and they had brought bags of throwables. Dean Rusk had told me about the tomatoes that had been tossed at him when he went on the Harvard campus. The kids at the Biltmore that night had sacks of grapefruit, which are easy to come by in Phoenix and are heavier than tomatoes. There was a surge in that crowd of kids and some of the city police moved over there fast.

Someone spoke to Paul. He was sixteen that year, but very smooth. The kids knew him because although "The Indispensables" stood for God, Mother, and the American Flag and you didn't admit to watching the show, most of them did watch it.

"You go over and tell them there's a reason behind all this," I heard someone say. "We don't want anything to start here."

Paul went over, and Cathy pulled herself together and followed him.

The security people were there by then, along with the police, but I truly believe it was Paul and Cathy who kept things cooled down. The security people could not have prevented those kids from lobbing their grapefruit if they had decided to go ahead, but no grapefruit got lobbed.

The senator made his speech and the event was over. We swallowed our pride, or rather my pride, and accepted the offer of the interview at the airport the next morning. In the car on the way home the kids and I decided that the Kennedy man was tired. Everyone in the party must have been tired. They were on the last day of a relentless, eleven-day tour.

The next morning at the airport Cathy and Paul did their interview. Paul talked about the reaction of the young people to Kennedy. Cathy talked about the reaction of one particular young person.

"You have a daughter about my age," she reminded the senator.

"That's right," he said.

"How does she feel about her father running for President of the United States?"

He smiled that famous smile. "I think she's very excited about it," he told her.

"Is your daughter afraid?" asked Cathy. "Are your children afraid?"

"I don't think so, really," he said. He stopped for a second, and he must have thought of that other Kennedy. "Oh, I suppose a little bit," he said. "I think she understands—I think all of my children understand—exactly what comes with the office, if I should be lucky enough to make it—the President of the United States, which is the strongest country in the world."

They were leaving on a commercial flight, and Ethel Kennedy, who knew all the TV signals at least as well as any director, began to make that cutting motion across her throat to tell him to hurry it up. They were holding the plane.

The kids presented him with one of the sweat shirts we give guests on the show. It was maroon, with "Indispensables" across the front in white letters. He laughed. "I wouldn't dare wear this in the senate," he said. "They'd think I was trying to . . ."

He stopped.

Ethel waved and sawed.

He never did say what the other senators would think about an Indispensables sweat shirt. He said a quick good-bye, climbed aboard the plane, and they were gone.

A few weeks later there were primaries in California. There was a victory celebration at the Ambassador Hotel there, and a man named Sirhan Sirhan waited outside the ballroom with a gun.

Cathy and Paul went on the air after the assassination and talked about it together. Cathy was controlled, always, but she did have tears on that show. Paul had to lend her a handkerchief.

They were able to draw one small ray of comfort from that terrible tragedy. It had, they decided, drawn us all together, if only for a little while. We all had mourned.

14

Some Interviews
You Don't Get

"They're losers," said Melvin Rogers. "That is, they're losers
unless we can find a way to help them."

Mel's wife, Betty, confirmed it. "The throw-away children,"
she told me.

We were in the library of the Leafcrest Girls Home, an
imposing structure that sits in one of the better parts of town
and pretends to be a private residence, which it once was. I had
been invited to dinner there because Betty and Mel, who run
the home, like to have friends in once in a while. Who doesn't?
No matter how deeply you are concerned with the welfare of
teen-age girls, you need to visit with your contemporaries occasionally. "Besides," Mel had said, "it's good for the girls to meet
new people. They get too shut in on themselves."

"You may be surprised when you meet them," Betty warned
me. "They're girls who have had everything—the wealthy families and the big houses, but no homes. The courts call them
incorrigible and their families can't handle them, so we get
them."

"They're very intelligent girls," said Mel, "but they're highly emotional. That's a dangerous combination."

Mel and Betty told me more about the girls. They did not enjoy exposing an incorrigible child, but you do not invite an acquaintance to meet twelve time bombs without issuing a warning or two.

All twelve residents of Leafcrest attended public school, which was the one touch of normality in their lives. What we think of as normality ended right there. Nearly every one was under psychiatric care. There were several drug addicts, and these girls had been on hard drugs like heroin. There were at least half a dozen runaways a week, and Mel was an expert at rescuing his lost lambs from detention homes and sometimes from the city jail.

I think, by the time we left the library and went into the living room, I was expecting twelve junior versions of Ma Barker. Betty was right. I was surprised. These girls came from the "best" families and they knew the rules about standing up when grown-ups came into a room. They knew about "How do you do?" and "Please" and "Thank you." There was too much eye makeup and the jeans were too tight, but they could pass the cookies and pour the fruit punch.

And once having done this, the twelve retreated. They sat on the floor around a huge coffee table, which Torquemada would have loved, and talked softly among themselves. Betty and Mel enthroned me in a magnificent Grand Rapids Inquisition chair and then sat across from me on the sofa. Conversation did not begin. We were aware of the girls putting on their show of ignoring us. We were aware that they were not ignoring us. Each had an invisible antenna out. They were sniffing me from a distance, the way wild things sniff a stray animal that wanders into their midst.

"I think," said Betty at last, "that Mrs. Black would like

some more punch. Would one of you girls take her glass?"

They didn't move, except to eye each other.

"I'm fine," I said quickly.

So much for the punch gambit. I decided to try the coffee table opening. "That's got to be the biggest coffee table I've ever seen," I said. "Anytime you can put twelve people around a table with plenty of room for elbows—"

"Who said anything about elbow room?" snapped one of the older girls. She had flaming hair and must have been almost eighteen.

A second girl laughed an unfunny laugh. "Red, you wouldn't have enough elbow room if you were alone in the Coliseum," she said.

I almost gasped. Whatever had happened to this girl, she had passed the point where you pretend things are pleasant when they're not. Some kinds of despair can, I suppose, produce total honesty—and blatant ill-manners, for the girl named Red had about two hundred pounds distributed in lumps and rolls and billows over her five-foot-five frame. With a muttered oath she heaved herself up. She wandered to the piano to grab a handful of cookies.

"Don't spoil your appetite," warned Betty Rogers. "Myrna fixed a good dinner tonight."

"Then why don't we eat it?" demanded a pretty young thing with big dark eyes. "I hate it when we have company. By the time we sit around trying to impress our guest, I lose my appetite. Then you all wonder why I'm so skinny."

Yes, I decided. Incorrigible is the right term.

An exceptionally lovely girl with long, blonde hair leaned on an elbow and glared. "If you're so skinny, Blackie," she wanted to know, "why do you keep telling us that everything you've got is in the right place?"

"You're jealous," retorted the girl called Blackie. "Flat in the front and flat in the back and flat in the head!"

"Wouldn't you like to show Mrs. Black your rooms before we eat?" asked Betty quickly.

They would not. They would rather poke each other with their elbows and grab for cookies and ignore the adults.

"Myrna did herself proud with these," said a girl with frosted hair as she bit into a cookie. "God, with a talent like hers, I wonder why she can't find a father for that baby of hers."

The other girls scowled at the frosted one.

Betty and Mel had told me of Myrna, an eighteen-year-old who did the cooking for the home. Myrna's background was different from that of the other girls. You can say that Myrna had no background. An orphan, she had been shoved from foster home to foster home and, at last, to the House of the Good Shepherd, where she gave birth to a strapping baby boy. According to Betty, that baby was a godsend to Myrna. For the first time in her life she had a reason to get up in the morning and breathe in and out all day. She had a reason to work. She had someone to give to. She brought the baby with her when she came to the Rogers. Her twelve neurotic housemates might make fun of her, but they loved her baby, so she was one of them.

The chilly silence got long, so I asked, "How big is this house?"

Mel waited, but none of the girls answered. Finally, "We have twenty-two rooms," said Mel.

"Just right for a prison," announced the girl with the frosted hair.

"You've got a big hole for a mouth, Zebra," said the blonde. She turned to Betty and Mel. "You know we don't feel that way."

"Hell, no." Red rested her huge bulk against the piano. "It's not what we would pick, but it's the best we've ever had."

A little mite of a thing with big blue eyes leaped in. "Hey, Mr. Rogers, I've got a big deal I want to talk to you about."

"Yes?" said Mel.

"Well, I've been real good lately," said that angelic child. "I mean, I stopped Red from knifing Zebra last week and I cleaned the kitchen while Myrna took little Buff to the doctor, and now I've got a favor to ask. I mean, for doing lots of nice things for everybody."

"What do you mean, everybody?" demanded the blonde. "You squealed on me when I just took a puff off a fag."

"That was to help, too," said the blue-eyed snitcher. "It helped you, Blondie. Didn't it, Mrs. Rogers?"

Betty Rogers stood up. "Let's eat," she said. "I can smell the roast."

"Fink! Fink! Fink!" said Blondie as we went into the dining room.

Dinner was not any cozier than the half hour with the fruit punch had been. The girls ate seriously and listened. Mel and Betty and I produced inanities about the weather and we talked about a couple of bond issues that had been defeated. When the plates were cleared away and Myrna brought in dessert and coffee she asked, "Do you smoke, Mrs. Black?"

"Sometimes, after dinner," I said.

Twelve heads snapped up. Twelve pairs of eyes looked at me as if I had just announced that I had to return to the detention home before bed check. Myrna disappeared into the kitchen and returned with an ash tray.

"How come she gets to smoke and we don't?" demanded Red.

"She's past eighteen, and she's a guest," said Mel quietly.

"We only get to smoke outside on the grounds," Blondie complained.

"You shouldn't smoke at all," I told them. "You're young enough to know better. I'm too old to have any sense where cigarettes are concerned. But if it's going to bother you, I don't need one now."

I wanted one very much.

"It won't bother us," said the girl with the big blue eyes—the good, good girl who did so much for everyone. "Mrs. Black, what do you think of *Hair*?"

"What?"

"*Hair!* You know, that play that's so big in L.A.?"

"Oh. I haven't seen it, but I understand it's quite interesting. Symbolic of lots of things."

"Do you think it'd be neat to go?"

"Yes, I'd like to see it sometime."

She zeroed in on Mel. "See, Mr. Rogers. See! That's the favor I wanted to ask. Because I've been really working at being good!"

"Sandy, save it for later," warned Mel.

"Just so you can say no later?" said Sandy. "You don't want to say no in front of your friend, do you? Huh?"

"Sandy! Later!"

Sandy got up and went around the table to perch on the arm of Mel's chair. Her hand dropped to Mel's shoulder and stayed there, moving ever so gently. "I don't want to be a problem, Mr. Rogers. I want you to be proud of me. You and Mrs. Rogers both. I'm just a mixed-up girl who's getting better because of what you've done for me—for all of us."

Betty Rogers had many saintly qualities, but she was a woman and she was human. She sipped her coffee and stared at that girl pulling the oldest act in the history of the female.

"The kids in my drama class are going and we'll be chaperoned and everything," Sandy cooed. "We'll go over on Saturday morning and come back Sunday. It's in two weeks."

"Big deal!" said Red. "Why should you go when we can't?"

"She'll take our clothes," warned Zebra, "and we'll get them back all sweaty and stretched."

"What do you care?" Sandy taunted. "You're not going to be wearing yours long anyway."

"Shut up!" shouted Zebra.

"Shut up what?" demanded Sandy. "If you're pregnant, you're pregnant. We all know it."

Zebra fled from the room, her napkin still crumpled in her hand.

Mel reached for the coffee and poured a second cup. "That was totally unnecessary, Sandy, and I think it takes care of your request. You're not going to L.A."

"Crap!" said Sandy. "Crap! Crap!" She went back to her own chair.

"You didn't have to tell that in front of Mrs. Black," said Blondie.

"Mrs. Black couldn't care less," Sandy replied.

"Zebra cares," said Blackie. "You know she's tried to kill herself before. Maybe now . . ."

Betty Rogers got up and went out of the room. In a moment, Mel followed her, not hurrying.

"Zebra'll be okay," said Sandy. It was the statement of a girl with a guilty conscience. She played with her spoon for a minute, then looked up at me. "You're doing real well," she said.

"How's that?"

"Most people who come here and don't know us don't last as long as you have."

"I haven't finished my dessert."

Sandy stared at me with curiosity and defiance. "So what do you think?" she said.

"About what?"

"About us? You feel like you're in a brothel or something?

When my mom comes to visit on weekends, she says she always has to take a bath after she gets home. Makes me feel keen about the whole thing."

"I don't believe I'll take a bath tonight," I told Sandy. "I usually have my bath in the morning."

I knew Betty and Mel were concerned with Zebra, but I did wish they'd come back.

"So what do you think?" said Sandy again.

"I have noticed one thing," I told her. "You call each other by colors instead of names."

There was a white-blonde girl, extremely pretty, and I hadn't heard her referred to as anything. "We don't use our names," she said. "You wouldn't either. We hate each other, you see. We look at each other and see how rotten we are and how sick we are. Who wants to identify with a bunch of rotten, sick people? Only we have to, so we hate ourselves, too. So, in a way, not using a real name is showing respect. Does that make any sense?"

"Aren't you being a little hard on yourselves?" I asked.

"Sometimes we like each other," Blackie admitted. "Like, we're all pretty good students, and when we bring home grades that are okay—and that's happened to all of us since we've been with the Rogers—we're kind of proud, and that's fun. Like, we're showing we can do okay, too, in our own way."

Betty and Mel returned with Zebra. Her eyes were red and swollen.

"Zebra, I'm sorry," said Sandy quickly.

"It's okay," said Zebra. "Except they don't know for sure if I'm pregnant, and I wish I'd kept my mouth shut. It'll be a big laugh if I'm not."

"It'll be a blessing," said Blackie. "It's a rough thing to go through."

"Let's don't compare labor pains again," said Blondie. Mel

cleared his throat, but not loudly enough to put the brakes on
her. "Seven of us have had babies, Mrs. Black," she said airily,
"and no greater or more amusing two hours can be spent than
hearing about our deliveries."

Sandy, still guilty after her attack on Zebra, changed the
subject. "Mrs. Rogers says you work for a television station.
Is it neat?"

"Yes, it is kind of neat. It's fun." I was relieved to get onto
something that wouldn't be so explosive. The girls pounced on
it. They asked about everything from TV production to the
real side of the "on the air" personalities. Then "The Indispensables" came into the conversation. I had hoped that the
show wouldn't be mentioned. I knew that to kids like these,
kids with terrible problems, "The Indispensables" might seem
kind of square.

I was right. My kids were square, square, square. The cracks
were witty and cutting, but they were revealing, too. Those
girls watched the show. They talked about various panels that
had been on. They knew what had been said. They talked about
the things they'd really like to see on the show. They mentioned
the music.

Then, out of a clear blue sky, Sandy asked if I'd like to see
her room. Well, Betty Rogers had suggested that before dinner.
I said yes, of course, and we all trooped away from the table,
leaving Betty and Mel to their coffee.

The house had been built in a huge square, with a patio and
a pool in the center. Each girl had her own room and bath,
and the rooms were beautiful. We came to Zebra's first and
she insisted that I come in and admire her fish. She had a huge
tank filled with bright, darting shapes, and each of the fish
had a name. Not a color, a name. There was Hushpuppy, who
sulked in the bottom of the tank, and Blackbeard, who was

nasty tempered, and Lady Godiva, who had long, filmy fins. "And here's Jimmy," said Zebra, taking a photograph from a bookshelf.

Jimmy wasn't a fish. He was a round-faced little boy of about ten. In the photograph, he was accompanied by the kind of idiotic-looking, shaggy dog all small boys adore. "Jimmy's my little brother," said Zebra, and there was real warmth in her voice. "That's Rags with him."

Of course it was Rags. What else would you call a dog like that?

"I have a brother, too," said Sandy. "Want to see his picture?"

We marched on toward Sandy's room. "You didn't have your cigarette," said Sandy. She made it sound as if I'd missed taking my vitamin pill.

"It's all right," I told her. "I don't need it."

"I can give you one."

"Sandy, you're not supposed—" began one of the others.

"Or I can give you a reefer, if you'd like," said Sandy.

Good little Sandy. Most helpful of girls.

"No thanks," I said.

Red sparked with interest. "You ever tried it?" she said.

I said no again.

"Why not?" asked Red. She moved close to me. Too close.

"It's really great." Sandy crowded in on the other side of me.

"If you've never really tried it . . . ?" Blackie left that thought hanging.

And they were all very close, standing in the hallway outside Sandy's room.

"Look," I said, "the stuff scares me."

"It scares everybody the first time," said Sandy. "I've got it in here. Come on in and try it."

And then Red had a switchblade in her hand. It was a pretty little knife with a pearl handle. It seemed too tiny for the massive Red, but it was a knife nonetheless.

I wondered whether I should yell for the Rogers or simply go along with the act and smoke the reefer. One reefer could not kill me, and I didn't need to inhale.

Then a puppy barked.

"Hey, Boojums!" One of the girls ran in through Sandy's room and opened the door that led to the patio. A gray white ball of fluff bounced in, wriggling all over, pink tongue out, and the girls forgot about reefers—and switchblades—and became twelve youngsters playing with a new puppy.

The dog had wandered in two days before. He came out of nowhere and no one had advertised in the Lost and Found. He wasn't housebroken and he probably hadn't had his shots and those girls loved him.

So the great reefer crisis was over. After the pup had been duly petted, admired, told what a good boy he was (I learned later that it was a female) and had settled down to nap on the foot of Sandy's bed, the conversation became general again. In the case of these tortured, troubled girls, that meant that they began to talk about themselves again.

"You could have a television series right here in this house," Blackie told me. "It would make 'Peyton Place' look like 'Romper Room.' "

I did not really want to know more about this, but Blackie told me. She said she had been raped by her father since she was four.

"Raped?"

"Well, forced intercourse," said Blackie.

I couldn't see the difference, but that must have sounded better to Blackie.

"Then last year I got pregnant," she said. "Not by my father, but I got pregnant and I was sent here."

Poor Zebra began to cry.

I had had enough. And on a full stomach. "The Rogers will wonder what happened to us," I said.

So Sandy put the pup back out onto the patio, since his education was incomplete, Zebra dried her eyes, and we want back to the living room.

The Rogers had fresh coffee waiting for me in the library. The girls stayed in the living room, a semicircle on the floor in front of the TV, and the Rogers and I had ten minutes to ourselves. Mel told me that what Blackie had said was true. "These girls have been destroyed by their parents," said Betty. "They're in the way at home, so they get swept under the rug."

What a panel they would make! I thought it, but I never in the wide world would have said it. But when I was leaving, the girls themselves said it. They wanted to be on TV.

You do have to consider the FCC and what you can do on the air and what you can't do. "What would you talk about?" I asked them.

"About life," said Red, "and how tough it is today."

"Do you think you could keep that kind of . . . general?" I asked.

Sure they could keep it general. They weren't dopes.

So the next week we took the cameras out to the home and did a half hour with the girls. They did not come on as Red or Sandy or Blondie or Zebra. They used their names—Janice and Penny and Louise and Jane and Ellie. We sat on the floor around that huge coffee table and talked. Not one of the girls mentioned her own personal problems, but they talked about parents—parents in general. They also discussed ecology, pollution, the Vietnam war, overpopulation, the generation gap, and how hard it was to figure right from wrong with the standards so mixed up.

"Parents are mixed up, too," said Janice, who had been Red.

Louise, who had been Blackie, completely agreed. "They're

as mixed up as we are," she decided. "And they've got so much guilt. Like, if you raise a kid who can't cope, who really can't cope, you feel guilty."

I thought of what Blackie had told me about her father that first night I visited the home. "If a kid can't cope," I asked, "isn't it the parents' fault?"

Blackie looked troubled. "Maybe. Yeah, sometimes I guess it is. But you can't let that stop you."

"What do you mean?"

"You can't just sit around hating your parents and blaming everything on them. You have to forgive them and go on from there or you'll never get anyplace."

"And have you?"

"Forgiven them? Yes. And I'm sorry. It's rough. Ever since the Second World War, everything's been changing. It's rough on them, too."

We ran overtime and it was hard to know what to cut. The girls were so good. Any parents would have been proud of them. They were intelligent, as Mel had said. They were also logical and fair. After that snappish, disgraceful dinner, it was hard to believe, but they had compassion. But then, I *had* seen them with the puppy. I had seen them stand up for Zebra. They cared. They cared about each other. They cared about their families. They were beginning to care about themselves, which might have been harder.

We did our editing and prepared to air the show. But first we had to get the approval of the judge who presided over the detention home where the girls had all spent time on occasion. He saw the film and approved it immediately—and with pride, he said. The board of the Leafcrest Home did the same. Then came the parents. They watched the show. They squirmed. Some of them stiffened and some of them cried. Some were astonished. They had never heard their daughters talk in such a candid way. Theirs had been a relationship of anger or apathy or frustration. Some of them were proud. No family names were mentioned, of course, and most of the parents signed releases. Then we had two holdouts. And then one. He never relented. He never signed. Destroy your daughter if you must, but don't let the neighbors suspect that she's in the Leafcrest Girls Home.

So the show was never aired. It was run at a symposium in Washington to demonstrate what such homes could do for "losers," but the television audience has not and will not ever see it.

Some interviews you get, and some you don't. That's the way it goes.

15

Black, White, Brown, Pink, Yellow

In Phoenix they called it *the trouble*. Los Angeles and New York and other cities had had their long, hot summers and eventually it was our turn. The pattern was classic. There were the disturbances in the streets, some sniping, some burning, some looting, and a great deal of fright.

I am pleased to report that I missed the whole thing. I was back in New York collecting an award for "The Indispensables." When I lugged the award back to Phoenix no one was a bit interested. One and all were busy talking about where they had been when certain shots were fired and certain stores were robbed or certain buildings were burned. Numbers of people who didn't own guns were buying them. Others who already had guns were cleaning them. We had become, like many American cities, a polarized community.

Polarization is one of those words. It used to be the exclusive property of the scientist. Now everyone uses it. It means that the older people have taken up residence in the north pasture while the younger ones swing in the south forty. It means that the conservatives are way, way over there to the right and the liberals are way, way over there to the left and heaven help the fence straddlers. It means black is beautiful and white is honky. It means *we* against *they,* whoever *they* may be.

I first bumped up against polarization back in Lansing, Michigan. I didn't know about polarization because I was eight years old. I only knew you weren't supposed to walk down that particular street because that was where the colored people lived. When I was eight, no one used the word black. But it was quicker to walk down that street on the way home from school than to go around by the socially accepted route. Besides, Bobby Johnson lived on that street and he was nice and he was in my class, so one day I walked down that street.

The black kids turned out a dozen strong and said "Yah! Yah! Yah!" at me.

"Yah! Yah! Yah!" is the same as honky. It means that you don't belong here.

I kept walking, not too fast, and one of the kids heaved a rock. Rock throwing is more contagious than smallpox. Instantly the air was full of stones. I ran. They ran after me. I held my lead until a tree root got in my way and I fell on my face. Then Bobby Johnson, who was a nice kid, and who was as black as any of the others and bigger than most, came galloping along like the Lone Ranger and ran them off. He walked me to the end of the street, admired my bloody nose, and told me never to walk that way again.

I never did. That's the nasty thing about polarization, or prejudice or bigotry or whatever name you choose for the thing that divides *them* from *us.* It cuts both ways. A ghetto is a place you can't get out of. When you shut people up in a place they can't get out of, it's childish to expect to be invited in for a visit.

There is one high school in Phoenix that has almost no white students. This is not because of any official policy. But white parents, even the most liberal ones, have withdrawn their children from the school. They had to. The black kids were showing their displeasure with the white community by dangling white students from a traffic overpass.

I had been a guest of that school long before the trouble in Phoenix. I was invited to speak at a graduation dinner for kids who had taken courses in journalism or TV or radio. The dinner was given in a not-quite-average motel complex where you could get a reasonably edible meal for $1.50. There was a coke party beforehand. I had the bad sense to show up early. No one called me a honky and no one said, "Yah! Yah! Yah!" No one said anything. There wasn't a teacher in sight. The big naked room that no one had bothered to decorate for the occasion was crowded with blacks and Mexican-Americans. I got a coke and stood and held it and was ignored for half an hour. I was invisible. I didn't belong there, so I was invisible.

Minorities often complain that they are invisible. Those kids let me know how it felt.

After a miserable while, the journalism teacher who had invited me came in and collected me. "Been visiting?" he asked.

"Yes," I said. It would not have helped to explain that I had only been standing alone, holding a warm coke.

The teacher ushered me into the dining room and up to the head table. Other teachers joined us and we waited and waited. Finally the kids stopped milling around and sat down and the dinner, such as it was, was served.

While we ate, the teachers watched those kids, and one of them said something very softly. Another teacher added his two bits and a third said a nasty word. There was one fine teacher who wanted those kids to have the best of everything—the best of instruction and the fairest of chances. "They aren't getting a good deal," he told me. "So many of them could do a lot better than they're doing."

I would have had to be an idiot not to have known the reason, or one of the reasons. With a single exception, the teachers were afraid of those kids—afraid and therefore full of hate. Each of them would have given anything to have taught in another school—any other school. They couldn't get transferred so they were there, filling in their time, not ever quite doing what they were supposed to do, but waiting for their pensions. They didn't like the kids so the kids scared them and then they hated the kids and the kids were the ones who would pay for it. It would have taken a Solomon to figure out who shoved who first.

After dinner we had speeches. The kids had had their cokes and their food and they would have liked to be on their way, but you have to have speeches after these dinners. It's a rule. Some fairly outstanding souls got up and talked about success and bright futures. The kids discouraged these speakers as much as they could without actually hurling any chairs. They rubbed their plates on the tables and rattled their glasses so that the room sounded as if it were under attack by giant termites.

So these kids did not believe in success, and for them the future might not be bright. It may have been their own fault, but they were reacting to a reaction to a reaction to a backlash. They had feelings that had been fermenting for a hundred years. Now the cork was out of the bottle and those feelings were provoking fears that had been just under the surface for a hundred years.

So if they did not believe in success, they might be interested in failure. When I got up, I told them how I had been thrown off the newspaper in high school because I wouldn't play politics.

They were interested in failure. They stopped scraping their plates and rattling their glasses and waited for more.

"I went to college," I said. I hated to confess this; so few of these young people would make it to college. "I took radio and they put me through the wringer. They did it on purpose because you're never supposed to lose your cool while you're on the air. The first time I went on radio, they burned my script just before the show. The second time, they let me keep my script but they cut my hair. I used to have long hair and they chopped it off at the back while I was at the mike."

Hair is sacred. A couple of mouths dropped open.

"I kept on going," I told them, "because you're supposed to keep on going. So they cut the buttons off my dress. I had a corduroy dress with three buttons in the front. They cut off the top one and I kept going. Then they cut off the bottom one and I still kept going. Then they took hold of the middle one and they were about to cut that off. I yelled.

"So I flunked radio."

The kids laughed, and I told them I'd never had to make a dime in radio, which was lucky, since I'd been such a failure at it. But now, in television, the lessons I had learned in that radio course—a course I had flunked—were turning out to be the most valuable ones in my life. "But then," I admitted, "television is easier than radio. They can't cut the buttons off your dress while you're on camera."

I started to sit down.

"Why you telling us all this?" asked one black girl.

I stood up again. "Would you believe me if I told you I was terrific at age five and that I've been getting greater ever since."

They laughed again and a boy got up. "When they took your column away from you in high school, did you hate them? Did you hate the teacher, or whoever did it?"

No one wants to admit to hate. It is an ugly emotion. I hesitated on that one. "I suppose I did then," I told them. "Fortunately, as you get older, you get over hate."

"Did you feel like quitting school?"

When that question was asked, I felt that at least some of those kids were with me. I told them there were lots of times when I wanted to quit school. Don't all kids have times when they want to quit school?

"How do you get over hate?" one of the girls asked.

"The way you get over any sickness," I said. "You have to go through stages when you've been hurt. At first you can't believe it's happened to you. Then you believe it and you get bitter. You hate. Then you bargain for some kind of return. Finally you can accept what's happened. You get well."

"The hate's the worst part," said one of the boys. "And what if rotten deals keep coming up? How many can you take?"

That was a question that can't be answered. They say that no one is given a heavier burden than he can carry, but this is not always true. The only thing I could suggest to those kids was a concept we'd worked out in that Sunday school class I had. One year, when we talked about suicide, the kids decided that you need a scale. You put on one side what's going for you and on the other side what's going against you. If what's going against you weighs heavier, you check it out. Is it truly all that bad, or are you fighting it the wrong way? Is hate the way to fight anything? If you hate and stay mad, you could have problems all your life. But then, that is exactly what some people want.

By the time it ended, I'd been on my feet for over an hour. The chairs scraped back and the teachers disappeared and the kids started milling again. One very big boy came up and touched my arm.

"I was on 'The Indispensables,' " he said. "Remember me?"

I didn't, but I could guess by his size. "Football?" I asked.

"That's right. I didn't like you."

I told him I was sorry.

"I didn't like you then and I don't think I like you now," he said. "But maybe, if you were black, maybe then I'd like you."

It was an honest remark. At least he didn't tell me that some of his best friends were white.

After the trouble in Phoenix there were more honest remarks. The black kids talked more. I planned a panel on racial unrest that fall. I had two white kids who bent over so far backward to be polite to the blacks that they were downright dull. They wouldn't argue about anything. I had a black boy who was militant, brilliant, and very angry and a black girl who was beautiful, articulate, and very troubled. The young people met with me the night before we were to tape the panel. The black boy was in a rage. He tried to cover it up with a show of humor, but that soon slipped. He didn't believe the black people had been given any chances. "No more than a hundred years ago, baby," he told me. "And it's your fault—you and your generation."

I agreed, but I couldn't agree that no progress at all had been made. Neither could the black girl. She was the only one of the kids who would argue with him.

He said violence would always be necessary if the black man was going to keep up with the white man.

She said violence was wrong.

He said the blacks were long overdue on being equal and leaders.

She said individual blacks had to prove their ability to lead.

He turned on me and said, "You owe us top positions in society and in business and government. That's a back payment. We've got it coming."

"But everybody has to prove himself," I told him. "Everybody!"

"Not us soul brothers, baby," said the boy.

"You're a good example," I told him.

"Me? Make sense, white lady."

"You're student body president of one of the largest high schools in the country," I reminded him. "You wouldn't have that spot if you hadn't proven to your peers that you're a leader."

He had to admit that this was true; it made him furious to have to admit it. He equated "The Indispensables" with the white Establishment, which was neither fair nor true. He sounded as if he wanted to burn down the world. Finally he stormed off on his own, leaving the girl to get back to the south end of town as best she could. I offered to drive her.

"You'd better not," she said. "I can grab a bus."

"But it won't be any trouble."

"You'd better not."

"I'm not afraid," I told her.

She was afraid, though it had been weeks since the trouble.

"Look," I said, "I've been down in your neighborhood at night before. The first year I was here I went to a meeting out near South Mountain. I had to slow down to take a corner and about sixteen kids jumped on the hood of my car."

There! That would convince her how tough I was.

"Weren't you scared?"

"Yes, a little bit. But I talked to them and they got off."

She laughed. "What are the magic words?"

She let me drive her part of the way. We headed down Central Avenue and she was quiet for a time. Then she said, "I really do hate violence."

"Yes?"

"I do. It's all wrong. It's so wrong how can anything good come out of it? Only now, when we walk down the street two or three abreast, people make way for us. And people even hold doors open for us. I suppose it's dumb, but I like that."

"Why do you think they do it?" I asked her.

"It's only since Watts and since the trouble here," she said. "So I hate violence, but maybe it's the only thing that's gotten us anywhere."

She made me stop the car about a mile south of downtown. She got out and waved and walked away, carrying her dilemma with her. What do you do when you hate violence, but it's the only thing that seems to work?

I don't know the answer. I can't believe that it's cleaning guns. Not on either side. No way.

If we could talk more? Angry as that black boy was, he showed up for the taping the next day. He wanted to talk.

If we could listen more? He didn't want to listen.

If we could make way more? It's still a big country. Surely there's room for everyone.

And what's bad about being black? Or white? Or brown or pink or yellow? You need all these colors to make a world.

16

Remember, Remember!

The summer of 1970 was a long, hot summer, and by 1970 we had grown accustomed to long, hot summers. But 1970 was different. The long, hot summer happened after a long, hot winter. There had been the Moratorium the October before, and we had gone onto the ASU campus to cover it. In a way it was wonderful to see all those young people protesting the war that no one wanted—the war that no one understood. And they protested peacefully. But then there was the SDS kid. He spotted the cameras and made himself available. Peaceful he was not.

He wanted to do away with the police. He didn't explain how. Just get rid of them.

And the military.

And, come right down to it, the government.

Bill Heywood was interviewing him. Bill is a pro and he can control himself under any circumstances. He controlled himself when he talked with that boy, but he was angry and it showed.

And what, Bill wanted to know, would the kid put in the place of that government he planned to wash down the drain?

Easy. A word. Socialism.

Bill asked him if he had ever been "over there." He hadn't, but he wanted to go.

I felt like saying, "Why don't you? Go ahead. Who needs you?" I felt like saying other rude things, like the rude things you read on some bumper stickers. I didn't. It was just as well. Demonstrations, however peaceful, are very touchy. Let one thing go wrong and POW!

Things had gone very wrong at Kent State, and we were mourning four beautiful young people from Kent State as we started the summer of 1970.

Things had gone wrong at Isla Vista, and the Bank of America was groggily rebuilding a branch that had been burned down.

So we roared into the summer and the schools closed and the kids went home—or to other places—and "The Indispensables" went off the air, as per schedule. I started on a show called "Young Ideas"—a summer replacement.

We had many young people and they had many ideas. We had panels on Vietnam, of course. We had panels on ecology, and the kids were uptight. We had only ten years to pull up our socks and do right or we would be dead.

Kids talked about the population explosion. One kid, a former Indispensable, came back from his first year in college with the solution to the population explosion. You sterilized everyone after they had two babies. You also kindly and quietly disposed of a lot of the folk we have now. Shades of Dachau!

Then there were the two young charmers who had a completely new twist on the population thing—or perhaps it was on the Women's Lib thing. They did not necessarily believe that every girl should be married. What they did believe was that every girl should have at least one baby *before* she was married. It was her right. I thought there was an obvious flaw in this line of reasoning. No one had a chance to consult the babies ahead of time. Would they enjoy being illegitimate?

All through the summer there were the reports. We had reports of rangers in Yosemite, riding through clouds of marijuana trying to clear a mountain meadow. We had reports from New York of rats in the streets and of automobiles left to rot and rust along the parkways. We had reports of desperate souls here, there, and everywhere who went into the bomb business and proceeded to blow up themselves, others and a few buildings—including one at the University of Wisconsin. We had the report on the fine young man who was killed in that bombing.

One Sunday morning, as the long summer was waning, I sat alone in the house and listened to the airconditioner make its cooling noise and thought of the kids packing their books and their shabby jeans and their tattered jackets, getting ready to go back to school for another year. I remembered the good old days in Great Falls and how complicated things had seemed to me at that time and how delightfully simple they seemed now that I looked back on them. I feared that the sky was about to fall.

Then the telephone rang.

I hardly had time to say hello. "Mrs. Black?" It was a big voice on the other end. "Mrs. Black? Jane? Hey, you still have the recipe for that crazy dip?"

Dip? Crazy dip? My mind thrashed frantically.

"You know," said that big voice on the phone. "That shrimp thing with all the stuff in it?"

It clicked. The shrimp dip. The kids eating potato chips and dip in the house back in Great Falls. George! That big voice was George!

"Where are you?" I was so excited that I squeaked.

"At the airport."

"In Phoenix?"

"In Phoenix. You going to be home? Can I come out and see you? I've got a surprise."

"I'll come and get you," I said quickly.

"You want to ruin my surprise? You stay where you are. I'll get a cab."

He hung up before I could argue about it.

I didn't waste time checking the kitchen. I knew there wasn't a can of shrimp in the house. I flew out to the car and over to the market and was back in ten minutes. I was furiously mashing shrimp when the cab pulled up.

I goggled through the window as George got out. It had been four years. He had written, but it had been four years since I'd seen him. He was now, to use a frontier phrase, a man grown. But he was still George.

And he was not alone. He was helping someone out of the cab. I saw a neat little hat and a neat little outfit that matched the hat and a very neat pair of legs. It was a neat little airline stewardess.

I didn't wait for them to ring the bell. I had the front door open as George guided that neat little person up the walk.

"Surprised?" said George. "So was I. I found her at the luggage pickup. Small world, huh?"

Did I know her? Was I supposed to know her? There was blonde hair, trimmed short, and wide eyes, very blue, and "Ah do declare, Mrs. Black!" said that neat little person.

"Davie!"

We touched cheeks, lady fashion, and then she laughed and hugged me, little-girl fashion. George hugged both of us together. They came in and I closed the door so that the heat couldn't follow them.

"Davie, where have you been?"

"All over," she said. She pulled off her hat. It made a difference. She was again Davie, beautiful Davie of the Sunday school class. Only she looked so much happier than I remembered. "I've been with the airlines a couple of years. I have twelve hours here, and I go back to New York tonight. I was looking in the phone book, trying to find your number, and this guy came up."

George had instantly appropriated the sofa and was slouched on his shoulder blades, grinning hugely.

"I thought he was one of those guys—you know," said Davie. She wrinkled her perfect nose. "Only it was Georgie!"

"No one *ever* calls me Georgie any more," he said.

"You mind if I do?"

"Not if it makes you happy," said George.

I got them cokes and finished the dip. George plunged into it with the potato chips and his eyes watered right on cue. "Mad!" he said. "Really clears the old sinuses!"

George, it turned out, had also been all over that summer. He had been home to Great Falls, and then had gone to San Francisco and to Los Angeles; he had arranged for a layover in Phoenix. He'd finished four years of premed at Harvard and one year of medical school, and now he was hesitating and pondering his future. "I may not finish med school," he told us. "I'm not sure. I may go into media. You know, I think I got hooked on media when we did 'The Indispensables.'"

"But we need doctors," protested Davie.

"Need good people in media, too," said George. "Jane, this dip tastes almost like it used to."

"I may have left out a thing or two," I told him. "It's been a long time."

"Remember Polly?" said George.

How could one ever forget Polly?

"I saw her when I was on the coast. She's okay. She married a nice guy and she has a baby. Terrific baby. Looks just like Poll."

"A little girl, isn't it?" I asked.

George frowned.

"It's a girl," said Davie firmly. "She's eight months old now.

I see Polly whenever I can—whenever I fly to Los Angeles."

"I was worried about Polly for a while," I said. "I understand she got bitter."

"She did," said George. "We talked about it. She wondered why did it have to happen to her and why did her parents have to die and like that. But she's past that now. She figures you can't expect life to be 100 percent fair. You've got to expect some bad breaks. She's a good kid. She reminds me of my mom."

"And how is your mom?" I asked.

George smiled. "Terrific. You know Mom."

I did know his mom, and she was terrific.

"You know, I was mad at her for a while," admitted George. "My first year at Harvard, wow, was I mad at her and Dad. You, too, I guess, Jane. All adults. I thought you'd really made a mess of things."

"First year away's hard," I said.

"You can say that again. Later I figured my folks hadn't made a mess of things at all. I don't believe I could do as well as they did. It was Mom, mostly. You know, she didn't have an easy time when she was a kid."

I knew that. George's mother had come from simple people.

"That may be what made the difference with Mom," said George. "She wanted us to have everything we needed, but she didn't want us to have everything we wanted."

Davie did not mention her mother. Instead, after a moment, she asked whether we remembered Bart.

"Sure do," said George.

"What ever happened to him?" asked Davie.

"I saw him at Berkeley," George told her. "He's way, way out. You remember how his folks were with him? I don't believe anybody ever said no to him in his life. He had everything—but everything! Well, he can't stand his folks now.

You'd think his father was Dracula and his mother was the bride of Frankenstein. He hates them. He hates everybody. He's as sour as a bad grape. He didn't want to hear one good word about anybody. Like I tried to tell him about Suzie. He couldn't care less."

"What about Suzie?"

"Well, no big thing maybe, but she's married. She met this guy in college in Montana and she married him. She has a baby, too."

"I always thought she and Bud . . ." I began.

"They did stick together like two slices of sandwich bread," said George. "Too much, I guess. She was like his kid sister."

George said he had seen Bud that spring in Boston. He was out of college and considering law school. Bud's favorite stepfather had been a lawyer.

"Say, what about Jake?" asked George suddenly. "The chauffeur. Davie, do you keep in touch with old Jake?"

Davie folded her hands and looked down at them and smiled. "He doesn't drive any more," she told us. "He's got real bad arthritis." Then she blushed. "But he's flying to New York next week. He's coming to—uh—to my wedding."

"Wedding?" I cried.

"You didn't tell me," said George. "Who? Somebody you met in New York?"

Davie absolutely glowed. "An artist. He's a good commercial artist, and he's a good painter, too. We're going to have a real teeny wedding, but it will be nice. My roommate's standing up with me and Bill's brother's going to be best man, and Jake's coming. It'll be in church, of course. Jake wouldn't like it if I didn't get married in church."

"No, he wouldn't," said George.

We sat and stared at Davie, who sat and stared at her hands and blushed and glowed and George finally asked if she'd have room at the teeny wedding for one more guest. "I can be in New York next week," he volunteered.

"Oh, Georgie, could you? Oh, I really would like that."

George wrote down the date and the time and the name of the church, and Davie's telephone number, and he said he'd meet the plane when Jake got in. But Davie wanted to meet that plane herself.

They asked about Jamie, then, and Jack and Tommy. They were glad that Jamie was keeping house for her new husband and that Jack was in Colorado Springs and Tommy in Germany. They asked about "The Indispensables."

"Off for the summer, of course," I told them. I told them about "Young Ideas," a show I was producing with Paul Hughes as moderator.

"We taped a show on Vietnam yesterday. It'll be on this afternoon. Want to watch?"

George wanted to watch, and Davie was agreeable, so when the time rolled around we tuned in to the show.

On "Young Ideas" I usually had four kids on a panel. For that show I had only three. It seemed plenty. There was a young conscientious objector who had thirty-seven solid reasons why every boy should feel as he did. There were also a West Point graduate and a student from ASU who had served a year in Vietnam.

The conscientious objector was not basically religiously oriented. He was simply against killing anyone. The West Point boy came from a military family and he made no secret of the fact that he approved of the military, but he was rational about it. The third boy had gone directly into the service after high school. He had had a year in Vietnam and he was very sure about what he wanted—an education and a future. All three were intelligent, articulate, and—like most of the bright young people—very well read.

The panel got under way with a review of our situation in

Vietnam. The boy from West Point knew the entire history of the Asian situation; so did the veteran and the conscientious objector. The conscientious objector did not believe we belonged in that war at all. He said it was only a political chess game, and we were losing our boys and doing nothing to strengthen the South Vietnamese.

The other two agreed that our tie-in in Asia was too strong.

"Quiet panel," George commented.

"It hots up," I told him.

It hotted up immediately. The veteran said that our government was trying to do something about pulling us out of the war. That lit the fuse for the conscientious objector. He hit out so hard at the government and the military that even on the television set you could see the boy from West Point getting red around the ears.

"Anything about our country that you do like?" asked the West Pointer.

"Not very much," said the conscientious objector. "I don't like it when anybody dictates to me."

This got to the young veteran. "It looks to me like you're pretty independent," he said. "You're going to a college of your choice. You're taking the courses you want to take. You have a part-time job that you want and you're spending your money the way you want to spend it."

"I don't like the government breathing down my back," said the conscientious objector. "I want to live like *I* want to live. I want to be left alone to do as I choose. That's what this country's foundation was based upon. Freedom for the individual!"

It then got loud and very hot as the other two hopped all over that boy. They told him no one could do exactly as he chose. Sure there were problems, gross problems, but we were working on them.

The conscientious objector turned on the veteran. "You talk

pretty big!" he accused. "That's what a uniform does to a person. I'll bet you played war all the time you were growing up. I'll bet you could hardly wait to play soldier!"

"I wanted to be a doctor," said the other boy, "but I couldn't afford college."

"So you got drafted," said the conscientious objector. "Now can you honestly tell me you don't resent those years the military took out of your life?"

"I don't resent them," said the veteran. "Of course, I got lucky. I'm alive. But I was sent to the other side of the world and I got to see how other people live. Before I was in the service, I suppose I felt a little like you do. I was pretty critical of our country. But after seeing what other countries are like, I realized what we've got here in America. It may sound corny, but I became ultrapatriotic."

The conscientious objector didn't have a chance to answer that because the time was up. The commercial came on and I snapped off the set.

"Well?" I said to George.

"That's been coming on for a long time," said George.

"The patriotism?" I asked. "Or the do-your-own-thing?"

"The do-your-own-thing," said George. "Remember the second year of 'The Indispensables' in Great Falls? Remember the kid who burned his draft card on camera?"

"Near brought down the town, didn't it?"

George chuckled. "I'm sure you heard from lots of people. Remember 'Dear Abby?' She said we were an overindulged generation and we didn't have any respect for our elders and there'd be trouble. She was right; there is trouble. But Jane, all three of the boys on that panel were right. The conscientious objector was right. We shouldn't be in that war in Vietnam. How can you be in a war you won't win? He just made that dumb mistake you make when you lose your head in an argument. He made a statement he couldn't defend. Deep down he has to know you can't do exactly as you please. And the other boys were right, too. I think our government *is* trying to pull us out, and we need our government. We need the military. And we need the police. If we didn't have them, we'd be dead before morning. We do have freedoms, but nobody can be completely free. We all have responsibilities."

"Ah do declare!" said Davie. "Ah thought the minister preached the sermons around heah!"

George got red. "Davie, I thought you'd forgotten how to do that southern bit," he said.

"It's like swimming," said Davie. "You don't forget."

"Well, anyway," said George, "that's what the campus troubles are about—freedom, responsibility, do-your-own-thing. And don't think the campuses won't be boiling this year. The students see themselves as the conscience of America. And maybe we need a conscience."

"But they don't know," I protested. "They haven't lived long enough."

"No," said George. "They've only lived long enough to know that things aren't the way they're supposed to be. Sure, your generation was the depression generation and you grew up believing that the most important thing was to keep a job, keep your family going. I've heard Mom talk about men coming to the door—good men—looking for something to eat. So you're success oriented. But a lot of kids aren't. They don't believe you should compromise and have dirty air and filthy rivers so somebody can make money. We have to change our aims, only we're so big and everything is so interrelated that we can't change quickly. So the kids are frustrated."

"And we have riots on campuses," said I.

"We have riots on campuses. And grown-ups are afraid of the kids. They're afraid of change. Change means some people are going to get hurt. Like the guy who makes DDT. Is he going to hurt when it's banned? You know darn well. But the kids will keep shoving. They know so much about the problems. Remember, this generation has been weaned on mass communications. They've *seen* what's wrong. It's right there every day on the screens. Bang! They see some guy bleeding in Vietnam. They see busses turned over in the south. And the pollution! I've just been in Los Angeles. You could put the air there in cans and use it to plug leaks in drains."

"But does bombing a building prove anything?"

"Not a thing," declared George. "And it's a criminal act. Sure, there are revolutionaries in there working—anarchists. They'd be crazy if they didn't take advantage of the situation. But there can't be a real revolution. As I said, we're too big. It's too complex. But what scares me is the fear. Dissent is one thing, but when there's violence, there's fear, and that can lead to more violence. If it keeps up, we're going to wind up with a police state. If that happens, it won't matter what kind of a police state—right or left. Nobody will be happy."

"So what do you think the answer is?" I asked him.

"Talk," said George. "And listen. Communicate. Remember the Sunday school class? We communicated. Remember how we used to start out trying to top the other guy's funny story, and it would all work right back to us? So we solved some problems for ourselves.

"So maybe kids haven't lived long enough to know everything. Maybe you have things you can teach them. But maybe they have things to teach, too. They can solve problems. And most of them are still uncorrupted. I think they really care. You have to care, too. And you're older. Your generation should be wiser. You want respect, so you have to deserve it."

George had eaten his way clean through the potato chips. "Wonder if they'll feed me on the plane," he said.

"I'll feed you here," I promised. "George, can we be wiser?"

"It'll hurt," decided George, "but we'd all better try it. What are the statistics? Aren't 50 percent of the people in this country under twenty-five?"

"A lot must be under twelve," Davie put in. "Do we have to worry about them?"

"They'll grow up," said George. "We have to work it out together and stop lashing out at each other."

Davie sighed. "You know, Georgie, sometimes you remind me of Everett Dirksen. And sometimes you don't."

"I couldn't possibly be Everett Dirksen," said George firmly. "I am twenty-three."

"I'm sure Everett Dirksen was twenty-three once," said Davie. One couldn't dispute that.

Incredibly, after demolishing all that dip and all those potato chips, George ate a hamburger. Davie nibbled a raw carrot and I drove both of them back to the airport in the dusk. They laughed along the way. They remembered Mary and the ride in the pig truck. They remembered Doctor Brownell. They remembered Bud and Suzie dumping the liquor down the alley drain. They were so happy. They were so dear. The sky could not be falling.

George caught his flight home to Great Falls. Davie caught hers to New York and her wedding.

I cried all the way home. I would so love to have gone to Davie's wedding. Even if the sky is not falling, you are allowed to cry about weddings.